Copyright © 2024 by Blaze X. Maverick (Author)

All rights reserved. This book or any portion thereof may not be reproduced or used in any manner whatsoever without the express written permission of the publisher except for the use of brief quotations in a book review.

This book is copyright protected. This is only for personal use. You cannot amend, distributor, sell, use, quote or paraphrase any part or the content within this book without the consent of the author.

Please note the information contained within this document is for educational and entertainment purposes only. Every attempt has been made to provide accurate, up to date and reliable complete information. No warranties of any kind are expressed or implied. Readers acknowledge that the author is not engaging in the rendering of legal, financial, medical or professional advice. The content of this book has been derived from various sources. Please consult a licensed professional before attempting any techniques outlined in this book.

By reading this document, the readers agree that under no circumstances are the author responsible for any losses, direct or indirect, which are incurred as a result of the use of information contained within this document, including but not limited to errors, omissions or inaccuracies.

Thank you very much for reading this book.

Title: Culinary Harmony
Subtitle: Savoring Sustainable Gastronomy Across the Globe

Author: Blaze X. Maverick

Table of Contents

Introduction **6**
Table Set: Introduce global cuisine's cultural significance. 6
Personal Motivation: Share your motivation for exploring world food. 9
Universal Language: Emphasize food's role in fostering understanding and connection. 12

Chapter 1: Culinary Journeys **15**
Explore, Anticipate: Discuss the thrill of culinary exploration and diverse expectations. 15
Sensory Adventure: Explore the nuances of aromas, textures, and flavors. 19
Food Diplomacy: Discuss food's role in global diplomacy and understanding. 25
Unexpected Finds: Share memorable, surprising culinary discoveries from your travels. 31

Chapter 2: Historical Evolution of Cuisines **37**
Ancient Roots: Explore the ancient origins of global culinary traditions. 37
Trade Routes Influence: Discuss the impact of historical trade routes. 46
Culinary Revolutions: Highlight historical events catalyzing culinary transformations. 53
Migration's Culinary Impact: Explore how migration shapes global cuisine diversity. 61

Chapter 3: Iconic Dishes **66**
Cultural Cornerstones: Explore iconic dishes symbolizing cultural heritage and excellence. 66
Chef Legends: Introduce chefs influencing iconic dish creation and popularity. 71

Artful Plating: Discuss the aesthetics of iconic dishes and presentation. 76
Modern Twists: Highlight contemporary reinterpretations of traditional iconic dishes. 82

Chapter 4: Innovations and Trends 89
Cutting-Edge Techniques: Explore modern culinary innovations, including molecular gastronomy. 89
Sustainable Practices: Discuss eco-friendly practices shaping the culinary world. 95
Tech in Cooking: Examine the influence of technology on cooking methods. 101
Street Food Trends: Explore the resurgence and global impact of street food. 109

Chapter 5: Cultural Significance 115
Festival Feasts: Discuss food's role in cultural celebrations and festivals. 115
Symbolic Ingredients: Highlight ingredients with cultural and symbolic significance. 122
Culinary Customs: Explore unique culinary rituals and traditions worldwide. 128
Food Stories: Share stories and legends related to cultural dishes. 134

Chapter 6: Farm-to-Table Movements 139
Sustainable Origins: Explore the farm-to-table movement and sustainable practices. 139
Community Connection: Discuss how this movement fosters community connections. 152
Heirloom Preservation: Highlight efforts to preserve heirloom and indigenous crops. 162
Local Choices, Global Impact: Explore the global impact of supporting local practices. 170

Chapter 7: Culinary Crossroads **178**
Fusion Flavors: Explore regions where diverse culinary influences merge. 178
Border Influences: Discuss how borders impact culinary landscapes and flavors. 185
Cultural Convergence: Explore instances where cultural convergence shapes culinary diversity. 190
Challenging Traditions: Highlight culinary crossroads challenging traditional norms. 195

Chapter 8: Behind the Scenes **199**
Kitchen Dynamics: Explore the fast-paced, dynamic world of professional kitchens. 199
Masters at Work: Profiling Renowned Chefs and Their Impact on Culinary Innovation. 203
Heart of the Kitchen: Discuss Chefs' Emotional Investment and Resilience in Their Craft 207
Kitchen Stories: Anecdotes and Moments from Kitchens Worldwide 211

Conclusion **215**
Global Tapestry: Summarizing the Diverse, Interconnected World of Global Cuisines 215
Continued Exploration: Encouraging Ongoing Exploration of Global Culinary Diversity 220
Ever-Evolving Story: Reflecting on the Dynamic Nature of Global Cuisine Narratives 224

Glossary **229**
Potential References **232**

Introduction
Table Set: Introduce global cuisine's cultural significance.

In the vast and flavorful tapestry of our world, food emerges as a universal language, weaving together cultures, traditions, and histories. As we embark on this gastronomic journey through "Culinary Harmony: Savoring Sustainable Gastronomy Across the Globe," our table is set to explore not only the diverse tastes that grace our plates but also the profound cultural significance that accompanies every culinary creation.

Global cuisine is a captivating reflection of humanity's shared experiences, shaped by centuries of history, trade, migration, and innovation. It goes beyond mere sustenance, evolving into a rich mosaic that mirrors the values, celebrations, and everyday rituals of communities worldwide. To truly appreciate the depth of global cuisine, we must first understand its cultural underpinnings.

As we pull out a chair and take our seats at the global dining table, the aromatic blend of spices, the sizzle of pans, and the rich colors of ingredients transport us to kitchens across continents. This introduction serves as a gateway to the heart of "Culinary Harmony," setting the stage for a nuanced exploration of the cultural significance embedded in every dish.

In every corner of the globe, food carries a unique story, a tale of tradition passed down through generations. It serves as a symbol of identity, connecting individuals to their roots and communities. The way ingredients are selected, the rituals surrounding meal preparation, and the communal act of sharing a meal are all integral parts of this cultural narrative.

Our exploration begins with an acknowledgment of the cultural diversity that defines global cuisine. It's a celebration of the differences that make each dish unique, as well as the shared threads that unite us through the language of taste. Whether it's the aromatic spices of Indian curries, the delicate flavors of Japanese sushi, or the hearty warmth of Italian pasta, each dish speaks to a cultural history that extends far beyond the plate.

As we delve into the chapters ahead, we'll unravel the stories behind iconic dishes, trace the historical footsteps that shaped culinary landscapes, and peek behind the kitchen doors to witness the passion and dedication of chefs worldwide. But before we embark on this journey of flavors, it's essential to understand why global cuisine matters on a cultural level.

Food has an extraordinary ability to transcend geographical boundaries, fostering understanding and connection. It serves as a bridge, connecting individuals who may be separated by oceans but find common ground at the dining table. The act of breaking bread together is a gesture of shared humanity, transcending language and cultural differences.

In "Culinary Harmony," we celebrate the vibrant interplay of flavors, techniques, and traditions that create a symphony on our palates. This book is not just about food; it's an exploration of the cultural intermingling that occurs when diverse culinary traditions come together. It's an invitation to savor not only the tastes but also the stories that unfold with every bite.

As we turn the page to commence our journey through global cuisine, let the cultural significance of each dish resonate with you. Let the aromas evoke memories of far-off lands, and may the flavors on your plate be a testament to the shared human experience that transcends borders. Welcome to "Culinary Harmony," where every meal is a cultural voyage and every taste is a step toward a more interconnected world.

Personal Motivation: Share your motivation for exploring world food.

In the pursuit of culinary exploration, motivations often find their roots in personal narratives, experiences, and a profound love for the diverse tapestry of global cuisine. As the pages of "Culinary Harmony: Savoring Sustainable Gastronomy Across the Globe" unfold, it becomes essential to illuminate the personal motivations that breathe life into this journey, shaping the lens through which each chapter is experienced.

At the heart of this exploration is an innate curiosity, a desire to traverse the world through the lens of its kitchens, markets, and dining tables. The motivation to embark on this gastronomic odyssey is deeply entwined with a passion for storytelling, where each dish becomes a chapter, and every bite, a paragraph in the unfolding narrative of human connection.

The inspiration to delve into the diverse world of global cuisine is not merely driven by the allure of exotic flavors or the thrill of culinary discovery. It is rooted in a belief that food, beyond its role as sustenance, serves as a powerful conduit for understanding, empathy, and appreciation of cultures far and wide. This motivation is a beacon, guiding the exploration of cuisines beyond their immediate tastes, uncovering the layers of history, tradition, and community embedded within.

Growing up, the kitchen was more than a room for preparing meals; it was a space where stories unfolded, traditions were passed down, and the essence of culture permeated the air. This personal connection to the kitchen fostered a deep appreciation for the role of food in preserving and transmitting cultural heritage. It is this connection that propels the exploration of world food—a quest to unravel the stories that ingredients tell, the rituals that accompany preparation, and the communal spirit that arises when sharing a meal.

A pivotal motivator behind "Culinary Harmony" is the belief that food can be a catalyst for change. By understanding and celebrating the sustainability practices embedded in different culinary traditions, there is an opportunity to inspire a global shift towards more eco-conscious dining. The motivation lies in shedding light on the sustainable practices that chefs, communities, and individuals embrace to ensure that our collective culinary journey leaves a positive impact on the planet.

Beyond the personal, there is a recognition of the transformative power of food experiences. Each encounter with a new dish, every shared meal with strangers-turned-friends, adds a layer to the tapestry of one's own identity. The motivation is to extend this transformative power to readers, inviting them to step outside their culinary comfort zones and embrace the world on their plates.

As the author of this gastronomic exploration, the personal motivation extends beyond a desire to share knowledge—it is an invitation to join in the celebration of diversity, to savor the beauty of cultural interconnectedness, and to acknowledge the responsibility that comes with influencing the narrative of global cuisine.

The passion for world food is not a solitary pursuit but a shared endeavor to create a space where culinary enthusiasts, seasoned cooks, and curious readers can come together. It is an aspiration to create a literary table where conversations about sustainability, culture, and the joy of discovery flourish.

In essence, the personal motivation behind "Culinary Harmony" is a love letter to the world on a plate—a testament to the belief that through the exploration of global cuisine, we can transcend borders, foster understanding, and savor the rich, diverse flavors that make our world a truly harmonious culinary experience.

Universal Language: Emphasize food's role in fostering understanding and connection.

In the kaleidoscope of global cultures, where languages may differ and traditions may vary, food emerges as a universal language—a means of communication that transcends geographical boundaries and connects people on a profound level. As we embark on the journey through "Culinary Harmony: Savoring Sustainable Gastronomy Across the Globe," it is crucial to explore how food, beyond its taste and aroma, serves as a powerful vehicle for fostering understanding and forging connections.

Imagine a bustling street market in Marrakech, where the aroma of spices wafts through the air, or a lively kitchen in Tokyo, where sushi chefs meticulously craft each roll. In these scenes, food becomes the medium through which stories are shared, friendships are formed, and cultural exchanges occur. It is this universal language that binds communities together, allowing individuals to communicate, celebrate, and understand one another.

At the heart of this exploration is the recognition that the act of sharing a meal is a deeply ingrained human experience, an ancient ritual that has persisted across time and continents. Whether seated around a family dinner table or partaking in a communal feast during a festival, the shared act of breaking bread fosters a sense of unity, reinforcing the idea that, despite our differences, we are all part of a larger, global narrative.

Food, in its essence, is a storyteller. It narrates tales of land and sea, of agricultural practices passed down through generations, and of the hands that lovingly prepare each dish. In "Culinary Harmony," the emphasis is on understanding these stories and recognizing the shared threads that weave through the fabric of global cuisine. It is an exploration that goes beyond the surface of taste, delving into the narratives that unfold when diverse culinary traditions intersect.

One of the remarkable aspects of food as a universal language is its ability to facilitate cross-cultural dialogue. When flavors from one part of the world encounter techniques and ingredients from another, a dialogue ensues—one that speaks of cultural exchange, adaptation, and the beauty that emerges when diverse culinary traditions converge. Each dish becomes a conversation, a bridge that connects seemingly disparate worlds.

As we navigate through the pages of "Culinary Harmony," it becomes evident that food has the power to dismantle stereotypes and preconceived notions. When we share a meal with someone whose culinary background differs from our own, we embark on a journey of discovery, challenging assumptions and broadening our perspectives. Food, then, becomes a catalyst for breaking down cultural barriers and fostering a deeper, more nuanced understanding of one another.

The universal language of food is not confined to restaurant kitchens or home tables. It extends to the fields where ingredients are grown, the markets where they are traded, and the kitchens where they are transformed into culinary delights. In every step of this journey, from farm to table, there is an opportunity for connection—a recognition of the shared responsibility we have as custodians of the planet and its resources.

In "Culinary Harmony," the universal language of food is also examined through the lens of sustainability. The emphasis is not only on the flavors that unite us but also on the collective responsibility to nurture and preserve the environment. Through sustainable gastronomy, individuals around the world contribute to a shared dialogue on responsible food practices, recognizing that the choices made in one part of the globe ripple across borders, impacting ecosystems and communities.

Moreover, food transcends words, offering an avenue for cultural diplomacy. It serves as a tangible expression of heritage, a way for communities to share their stories and traditions with the world. Culinary diplomacy, explored in the pages ahead, showcases instances where food becomes a tool for building bridges between nations, fostering goodwill, and promoting international understanding.

In essence, "Culinary Harmony" is not just a celebration of flavors; it is an exploration of the universal language that binds us all through food. It is an invitation to savor the stories, embrace the connections, and recognize the profound impact that our culinary choices can have on a global scale. As we turn the pages, let us revel in the richness of this universal language, appreciating the diverse voices that contribute to the symphony of global cuisine.

Chapter 1: Culinary Journeys
Explore, Anticipate: Discuss the thrill of culinary exploration and diverse expectations.

In the world of gastronomy, embarking on a culinary journey is akin to setting sail into uncharted waters—a thrilling adventure filled with anticipation, discovery, and the promise of diverse flavors waiting to be unveiled. As we delve into the first chapter of "Culinary Harmony: Savoring Sustainable Gastronomy Across the Globe," we enter a realm where the exploration of global cuisines becomes a passport to an ever-expanding world of tastes and traditions.

The thrill of culinary exploration lies in the unknown, the excitement of stepping outside familiar culinary boundaries and embracing the unexpected. It's a journey that beckons us to wander through bustling markets, savor street food delights, and sit at tables where the air is thick with the aroma of spices and the chatter of diverse languages. This exploration is not just about the physical act of traversing distances; it's about immersing oneself in the stories that unfold with each dish.

As we set out on this journey, anticipation becomes a companion, fueling the senses with the promise of new and intriguing culinary experiences. The mere thought of tasting a dish that carries the essence of a distant culture, prepared with techniques passed down through generations, evokes a sense of wonder. It is this anticipation that transforms a simple meal into a gateway to cultural understanding, where each bite becomes a portal to the traditions and histories of a community.

Diverse expectations shape the lens through which we approach culinary exploration. For some, it's the quest for bold, spicy flavors that define the streets of Bangkok or the aromatic complexity of Middle Eastern cuisine. For others, the expectation may be rooted in the pursuit of delicate textures and umami notes characteristic of Japanese gastronomy. These expectations, diverse and multifaceted, serve as compass points guiding our culinary journey, each one leading to a unique destination on the global flavor map.

The anticipation and thrill of culinary exploration are not confined to the moment of tasting alone. It begins with the decision to step outside one's comfort zone, to be open to the unfamiliar, and to embrace the unknown with a curious spirit. This sense of adventure becomes a driving force, motivating individuals to seek out hidden gems, whether tucked away in a bustling metropolis or nestled in the quiet corners of a small village.

In "Culinary Harmony," the exploration goes beyond the mere act of tasting. It involves understanding the cultural contexts that give rise to specific flavors, ingredients, and culinary techniques. It's about uncovering the stories that unfold in kitchens around the world—the hands that lovingly prepare meals, the traditions that shape culinary practices, and the innovations that arise from the dynamic interplay of old and new.

An essential aspect of the thrill of culinary exploration is the element of surprise. It's the joy of stumbling upon an unassuming street vendor serving up a culinary masterpiece or discovering a hidden gem in a neighborhood known for its culinary diversity. These surprises, often unexpected and delightful, add layers to the journey, transforming it into a treasure hunt where every corner turned reveals a new and exciting gastronomic experience.

Moreover, culinary exploration is an exercise in breaking down preconceived notions and challenging culinary stereotypes. It involves questioning assumptions about what defines "authentic" cuisine and recognizing that the beauty of global gastronomy lies in its diversity. The thrill is in experiencing firsthand how culinary traditions evolve, adapt, and fuse with other influences, creating a dynamic and ever-changing landscape of flavors.

The diverse expectations that accompany culinary exploration also extend to the interactions with the people behind the food. It's about connecting with chefs, artisans, and home cooks whose stories are woven into the fabric of their culinary creations. It's the anticipation of learning from those who have dedicated their lives to preserving traditional techniques and the excitement of witnessing how their craft evolves in contemporary kitchens.

In "Culinary Harmony," the exploration encompasses not only the well-known cuisines celebrated on an international stage but also the hidden gems that may not yet have received widespread recognition. It is an acknowledgment that every culture, no matter how small or seemingly obscure, contributes to the rich mosaic of global cuisine. The thrill lies in uncovering these lesser-known culinary traditions and shedding light on the culinary diversity that exists beyond popular narratives.

As we navigate the diverse landscapes of culinary exploration, the significance of anticipation becomes clear—it is the fuel that propels us forward, encouraging us to seek out the unfamiliar, embrace the unexpected, and approach each culinary encounter with an open heart and an eager palate. The thrill of culinary exploration is an ongoing journey, where every meal is a chapter in a larger narrative of global flavors, traditions, and the shared joy of savoring the world on a plate.

Sensory Adventure: Explore the nuances of aromas, textures, and flavors.

Embarking on a culinary journey is, at its core, a sensory adventure—a symphony of aromas, a dance of textures, and a celebration of flavors that resonate with the soul. In the pages of "Culinary Harmony: Savoring Sustainable Gastronomy Across the Globe," we delve into the intricacies of this sensory voyage, where every dish becomes a canvas, and every bite is an exploration of the diverse and enchanting world of global cuisine.

Aromas: A Prelude to Flavor

The journey begins with the olfactory senses—a prelude to the culinary experience that awaits. Aromas have the power to transport us across continents, evoking memories of distant lands and hinting at the flavors that will soon grace our palates. The streets of Marrakech come alive with the intoxicating scent of cumin and coriander, while the air in a Parisian patisserie is infused with the fragrance of buttery pastries. In "Culinary Harmony," the exploration of aromas is an integral part of the sensory adventure, a journey into the heart of cultural expression through scent.

The nuances of aromas extend beyond the individual ingredients; they tell stories of culinary techniques, regional influences, and the traditions that shape each dish. It's the smoky aroma of a barbecue in the southern United States, the heady perfume of saffron in a Persian rice dish, and the comforting scent of spices in an Indian curry. As we navigate the global flavor map, the aromas become guideposts, leading us to the heart of culinary traditions and the essence of a community's identity.

The sensory adventure of aromas also involves understanding the art of spice blending, a skill perfected by generations of spice merchants and chefs. From the complex garam masala of Indian cuisine to the aromatic za'atar of Middle Eastern dishes, each spice blend tells a story of cultural heritage, trade routes, and the meticulous craftsmanship passed down through families. Exploring these aromas is a journey into the spice bazaars, where vibrant colors and intoxicating scents converge to create a sensory tapestry.

Moreover, the anticipation of aromas is not limited to the savory; it extends to the world of desserts and pastries. The sweet scent of vanilla beans in a French patisserie, the warm aroma of cinnamon in a Scandinavian bun, and the tropical fragrance of coconut in a Southeast Asian dessert—all contribute to the sensory symphony that accompanies our global culinary exploration. Aromas, in their diversity, become a language of their own, communicating the essence of a dish long before it touches the lips.

Textures: The Dance on the Palate

The sensory adventure continues with the exploration of textures—a dance on the palate that adds dimension to the culinary experience. Each cuisine contributes its unique choreography, offering a repertoire of textures that range from crisp and crunchy to tender and melt-in-the-mouth. In "Culinary Harmony," the appreciation of textures is an invitation to savor the tactile delights that elevate a dish from a mere meal to a multisensory celebration.

The crisp crackle of a freshly baked baguette, the velvety smoothness of a well-made risotto, and the satisfying crunch of a perfectly fried spring roll—all engage the senses in a dance that goes beyond flavor alone. Textures, in their diversity, become storytellers, revealing the craftsmanship of chefs and the cultural preferences that shape culinary traditions.

Understanding textures is also a journey into the world of culinary techniques. It's the mastery of a chef who skillfully balances the crispy exterior and tender interior of a tempura, or the artistry involved in creating the intricate layers of a French mille-feuille. From the al dente perfection of Italian pasta to the silkiness of Chinese dumpling wrappers, the textures in global cuisine are a testament to the skill and creativity that chefs bring to their craft.

Exploring textures is not only about the physical sensations on the palate but also about the emotional response they evoke. The comforting softness of a bowl of risotto can transport us to the hearth of an Italian kitchen, while the crackling crispness of Korean fried chicken conjures images of bustling street markets in Seoul. In "Culinary Harmony," textures become a means of connecting with the cultural stories embedded in each dish, fostering a deeper understanding of the communities that have perfected the art of culinary texture.

Moreover, the adventure of textures extends to the diversity of ingredients used in global cuisine. The chewiness of rice cakes in Japanese mochi, the silky mouthfeel of coconut milk in Southeast Asian curries, and the hearty bite of quinoa in South American dishes—all contribute to the rich mosaic of textures that define culinary traditions around the world. Each bite becomes a tactile exploration, an invitation to appreciate the varied landscapes of the global palate.

Flavors: A Symphony on the Tongue

At the heart of the sensory adventure lies the exploration of flavors—a symphony on the tongue that encompasses the sweet, the savory, the sour, the bitter, and the umami. Flavors, in their complexity, are the protagonists of our culinary journey, each one telling a story of culinary heritage, local ingredients, and the harmonious balance achieved by skilled hands. In "Culinary Harmony," the exploration of flavors is an odyssey into the essence of global cuisine, where every dish is a composition of diverse tastes and cultural influences.

Sweetness, a universally cherished flavor, takes on myriad forms in global cuisine. From the honeyed notes of Middle Eastern baklava to the rich sweetness of Brazilian brigadeiros, each culture contributes its unique interpretation of this beloved flavor. The symphony of sweetness extends to the world of fruits and desserts, where the nuanced sweetness of tropical mangoes in Southeast Asia contrasts with the delicate sweetness of European pastries. Exploring the diverse expressions of sweetness is a journey into the cultural preferences and natural bounties that shape global culinary traditions.

Savoriness, often associated with umami, adds depth and richness to dishes across continents. The savory umami notes of soy sauce in Japanese cuisine, the robust savoriness of French bouillabaisse, and the complex umami profile of fermented foods in Korean kimchi—all exemplify the varied expressions of this fundamental flavor. The exploration of umami is a journey into the alchemy of ingredients and the transformative power of culinary techniques that enhance the savory experience.

The adventure of flavors also embraces the sour, a palate-tingling sensation that adds brightness and complexity to dishes. The zesty sourness of Mexican ceviche, the refreshing tartness of Indian tamarind chutney, and the citrusy acidity of Mediterranean dishes—all contribute to the global symphony of flavors. The exploration of sour notes is a voyage into the world of acids and fermentation, where culinary traditions harness the transformative power of sour ingredients.

Bitterness, often a misunderstood flavor, takes center stage in certain culinary traditions, offering a counterpoint to sweetness and enhancing the overall flavor profile. The gentle bitterness of Italian radicchio, the robust bitterness of Ethiopian coffee, and the earthy bitterness of dark chocolate all contribute to the rich tapestry of global flavors. Exploring bitterness is an invitation to appreciate the complexity and balance achieved by chefs who masterfully incorporate this often-overlooked flavor into their creations.

In "Culinary Harmony," the adventure of flavors extends to the exploration of spices and herbs—a diverse palette that enhances dishes with aromatic and nuanced notes. From the warmth of cinnamon in Middle Eastern cuisine to the fiery heat of chili peppers in Mexican dishes, each spice and herb contributes to the flavor symphony in its own unique way. The exploration is not just about individual spices but also about the harmonious blends that define the flavor profiles of different cuisines.

Moreover, the journey into flavors is an exploration of the cultural significance attached to certain tastes. It's understanding the reverence for the bitter flavors in traditional Chinese medicine, the celebration of sweetness in Indian festivals, and the cultural rituals associated with savory flavors in French gastronomy. Flavors, in their cultural context, become a language through which communities express their identity and heritage.

As we navigate the sensory adventure of aromas, textures, and flavors in "Culinary Harmony," each dish becomes a canvas painted with the brushstrokes of cultural expression. The symphony on the tongue is not just about taste; it's about the stories, traditions, and diverse influences that converge to create a culinary masterpiece. It's an exploration that invites us to savor the world on a plate, appreciating the nuances that make each dish a sensory journey through the global landscape of flavor.

Food Diplomacy: Discuss food's role in global diplomacy and understanding.

Food, beyond its role as sustenance, possesses a remarkable ability to transcend borders and foster connections between people and nations. In the pages of "Culinary Harmony: Savoring Sustainable Gastronomy Across the Globe," the exploration of culinary journeys extends to the realm of food diplomacy—a phenomenon where the shared experience of meals becomes a powerful tool for building bridges, fostering international understanding, and promoting a more interconnected world.

Culinary Bridges: Breaking Down Barriers

At the heart of food diplomacy is the idea that the act of sharing a meal can be a profound and universal form of communication. When individuals sit around a table and partake in the same dishes, cultural differences begin to fade, and a shared understanding emerges. Culinary diplomacy involves breaking down barriers and building bridges, allowing individuals to connect on a human level, irrespective of political or cultural divides.

The shared experience of food creates a common ground where diplomatic discussions can unfold more smoothly. Heads of state and diplomats often engage in "culinary summits," where the choice of dishes becomes a symbolic gesture of goodwill. From state banquets featuring traditional delicacies to informal gatherings where leaders share a casual meal, food serves as a medium for establishing rapport and fostering a sense of camaraderie.

A poignant example of culinary diplomacy lies in the concept of "gastrodiplomacy," where countries use their cuisine as a tool to enhance their image on the global stage. By showcasing their culinary heritage and inviting the world to savor their traditional dishes, nations can create positive perceptions that extend beyond politics. Gastrodiplomacy recognizes the potential of food to evoke positive emotions, making it a valuable asset in building international relationships.

Diversity on the Diplomatic Table: An International Feast

Culinary diplomacy embraces the rich diversity of global cuisines, reflecting the cultural wealth of nations. International gatherings, whether formal diplomatic events or cultural exchanges, often feature an array of dishes that showcase the flavors, ingredients, and culinary techniques unique to each country. The diplomatic table becomes an international feast, inviting participants to savor the world's cultural heritage through the language of taste.

Through shared meals, nations can express their identity and heritage, showcasing the diversity of their culinary traditions. The diplomatic table becomes a canvas where cultural narratives are painted with flavors and aromas. It's an opportunity for nations to extend an invitation to the world, saying, "Come, taste our history, our traditions, and the essence of who we are."

Moreover, the act of sharing food at the diplomatic table is symbolic of the shared responsibility nations have in addressing global challenges. Climate change, food security, and sustainable agriculture are just a few of the pressing issues that impact the world. By coming together over a meal, diplomats acknowledge their interconnectedness and the need for collaborative efforts to address these challenges. Food diplomacy thus becomes a conduit for fostering dialogue on shared responsibilities and promoting global cooperation.

Culinary Dialogues: Facilitating Understanding

Food, as a universal language, facilitates dialogues that transcend words. Culinary diplomacy involves more than just sharing meals; it's about creating spaces for conversations that promote mutual understanding. In diplomatic settings, breaking bread together allows individuals to discuss complex issues in a more relaxed and informal atmosphere. It softens the formality of diplomatic negotiations, fostering an environment where genuine connections can be established.

The act of preparing and sharing food also opens the door to cultural exchange. Diplomats who engage in culinary diplomacy often take part in cooking classes, food tours, or visits to local markets. These experiences provide insights into the cultural context of the cuisine and offer a deeper understanding of the traditions that shape a nation's culinary identity. As diplomats immerse themselves in these culinary experiences, they gain a more nuanced perspective that goes beyond political and economic considerations.

Additionally, culinary diplomacy extends beyond the diplomatic corps to involve citizens and communities. Cultural exchange programs, food festivals, and collaborative cooking initiatives bring people from different nations together. These interactions promote grassroots diplomacy, allowing individuals to learn about each other's cultures through the shared experience of preparing and enjoying meals. By fostering connections at the community level, culinary diplomacy contributes to a more inclusive and interconnected global society.

The Power of Culinary Stories: Shaping Perceptions

In the realm of food diplomacy, every dish becomes a storyteller, narrating tales of history, tradition, and the cultural evolution of a nation. Culinary stories have the power to shape perceptions and challenge stereotypes. When nations share their culinary heritage, they invite the world to see beyond political headlines and appreciate the richness of their cultural narratives.

For example, a country that is often portrayed negatively in the media can use its cuisine to showcase the warmth and hospitality of its people. By offering a taste of its traditional dishes, it provides an alternative narrative that humanizes the nation and fosters understanding. Culinary diplomacy becomes a tool for dispelling misconceptions and building bridges between cultures.

The power of culinary stories also lies in their ability to preserve cultural heritage. Many traditional recipes have been passed down through generations, and by sharing these dishes on the diplomatic stage, nations can showcase the resilience and continuity of their cultural practices. Culinary diplomacy thus becomes a means of preserving and celebrating the intangible heritage that defines a community.

Challenges and Opportunities: Navigating Culinary Diplomacy

While culinary diplomacy offers tremendous opportunities for fostering international understanding, it also presents challenges. The interpretation of certain dishes or ingredients can vary across cultures, and what may be considered a delicacy in one country could be met with reservations in another. Cultural sensitivities, dietary restrictions, and culinary taboos must be navigated with care to ensure that the diplomatic table remains a space of respect and inclusivity.

Moreover, the potential for culinary diplomacy to be seen as superficial or performative is a challenge that must be addressed. Genuine engagement in cultural exchange and a commitment to understanding the nuances of a nation's culinary heritage are essential for the success of culinary diplomacy initiatives. It requires diplomats to move beyond the surface of popular dishes and delve into the deeper layers of culinary traditions.

As technology continues to shrink the global landscape, culinary diplomacy also finds new opportunities in the digital realm. Virtual cooking classes, online food festivals, and social media campaigns allow nations to share their culinary stories with a global audience. These digital initiatives amplify the reach of culinary diplomacy, creating spaces for cross-cultural dialogue that transcend geographical boundaries.

Conclusion: The Diplomacy of Shared Plates

In conclusion, the role of food in global diplomacy is a testament to its power as a unifying force. Culinary diplomacy transcends political differences and fosters connections between individuals and nations. The shared experience of meals becomes a medium for building bridges, promoting cultural understanding, and shaping perceptions on the world stage.

As we embark on the culinary journey through "Culinary Harmony," the exploration of food diplomacy becomes an integral part of understanding the interconnectedness of global cuisines. Each dish becomes a diplomatic envoy, carrying with it the stories, traditions, and aspirations of the people who prepare and share it. Culinary diplomacy is a celebration of the diversity that makes our world rich, vibrant, and interconnected—a diplomacy of shared plates that invites us to savor the flavors of global understanding.

Unexpected Finds: Share memorable, surprising culinary discoveries from your travels.

Embarking on a culinary journey is akin to setting sail into uncharted waters, where every meal is a potential treasure waiting to be discovered. In "Culinary Harmony: Savoring Sustainable Gastronomy Across the Globe," the exploration of unexpected finds becomes a narrative thread, weaving through the tapestry of global cuisine. These are the moments of serendipity, where a chance encounter with a dish or a culinary tradition leaves an indelible mark on the palate and the memory.

A Street Food Odyssey: The Unassuming Gems

Some of the most unexpected culinary discoveries unfold in the bustling alleys and vibrant street markets that define the culinary landscapes of cities around the world. In Bangkok, the aroma of sizzling Pad Thai draws me to a humble street vendor tucked away in a narrow lane. The seemingly unassuming cart reveals itself as a culinary gem, producing a perfect harmony of sweet, sour, and spicy flavors that dance on the taste buds.

In Mexico City, a late-night exploration leads to the discovery of elotes, a street food delight featuring grilled corn on the cob slathered in mayonnaise, chili powder, and cotija cheese. The unexpected combination of creamy, spicy, and tangy elements creates a symphony of flavors that challenges preconceived notions of what street food can be.

These street-level encounters are a testament to the fact that some of the most memorable culinary experiences are hidden in plain sight. It's the small, unpretentious stalls that often hold the keys to authentic, unfiltered flavors—a truth that reveals itself only to those willing to venture off the beaten path.

Culinary Crossroads: Fusion and Unexpected Pairings

Culinary journeys frequently lead to crossroads where diverse culinary traditions intersect, giving rise to unexpected and delightful fusions. In the melting pot of Singapore, the discovery of Hainanese chicken rice sushi is a revelation. This unexpected pairing of Japanese and Chinese flavors creates a harmonious dish that encapsulates the cultural diversity of the city-state.

Similarly, in the Mediterranean, the fusion of Greek and Turkish influences results in the unexpected delight of moussaka-filled baklava. The savory layers of eggplant, minced meat, and béchamel sandwiched between flaky phyllo pastry challenge conventional expectations and showcase the inventiveness born out of cultural convergences.

These culinary crossroads become windows into the fluid nature of global gastronomy, where traditional boundaries blur, and unexpected connections form. They offer a reminder that the exploration of food is not confined to rigid categories but is an ever-evolving journey that embraces the unexpected.

Hidden Gems: Off the Beaten Path

Some of the most surprising culinary discoveries emerge from the depths of lesser-explored regions, where local traditions thrive away from the spotlight of popular tourism. Venturing into the heart of Oaxaca, Mexico, unveils the rich tapestry of mole varieties, each one a unique blend of spices, chilies, and chocolate. The complexity and depth of flavors in these regional specialties challenge the notion that Mexican cuisine is homogenous.

In the remote villages of Vietnam, a chance encounter with com lam introduces a traditional method of cooking rice in bamboo tubes. The smoky aroma and earthy flavor imparted by this unconventional technique elevate a simple staple to an unexpected delicacy. These hidden gems celebrate the diversity of regional cuisines that often remain obscured by more widely recognized dishes.

Exploring off the beaten path is not just a physical journey but a mindset—an openness to embrace the unfamiliar and celebrate the culinary treasures that emerge in unexpected corners of the world.

Ephemeral Delights: Seasonal Surprises

Seasonal ingredients play a pivotal role in the world of gastronomy, offering surprises that are as fleeting as they are extraordinary. In the Mediterranean, the arrival of white truffles transforms simple dishes into sublime experiences. The pungent aroma and earthy flavor of these underground treasures elevate pasta dishes to an unparalleled level of indulgence.

In Japan, the ephemeral cherry blossom season brings the celebration of sakura-themed sweets, where delicate cherry blossom petals are incorporated into traditional confections. The fleeting nature of these seasonal delights adds an element of anticipation and exclusivity, turning each encounter into a cherished memory.

Unexpected finds in the realm of seasonal ingredients underscore the dynamic relationship between food and nature. The awareness of the transient nature of certain flavors encourages a deeper appreciation for the culinary moments that arise only at specific times of the year.

Home-cooked Wonders: Invitations into Local Kitchens

Some of the most surprising culinary discoveries occur within the intimate setting of local kitchens, where home cooks generously share their cherished family recipes. In the heart of Tuscany, a spontaneous invitation leads to the revelation of the art of making pici—a hand-rolled pasta that embodies the soul of Italian home cooking. The simplicity of ingredients and the hands-on process create a connection to the essence of the region.

Similarly, in the vibrant kitchens of Kolkata, India, the preparation of roshogolla—a sweet treat made from fresh cheese balls soaked in sugar syrup—unfolds as a family affair. The sharing of techniques, stories, and laughter transforms the act of cooking into a cultural exchange that transcends language barriers.

Home-cooked wonders offer a personal connection to the heart of a culture, allowing travelers to go beyond the surface of restaurant menus and taste the authenticity that defines local cuisine. These experiences become invitations into the warmth and hospitality of local communities.

Revived Traditions: Culinary Resurrections

Certain culinary discoveries involve the revival of ancient traditions and culinary practices that have withstood the test of time. In the mountainous regions of Peru, the encounter with pachamanca—a traditional Andean cooking method using hot stones buried in the ground—reveals a culinary heritage dating back to pre-Incan times. The earthy, smoky flavors of meats, vegetables, and potatoes cooked in this ancestral manner transport diners to a different era.

Likewise, the resurgence of ancient grains such as quinoa in modern kitchens is a testament to the adaptability and resilience of culinary traditions. Once considered a staple of Incan diets, quinoa has found its way onto plates worldwide, embodying a sustainable and nutrient-rich alternative to more common grains.

Revived traditions speak to the cyclical nature of culinary innovation, where the past becomes a source of inspiration for the present. These culinary discoveries not only honor the legacies of the past but also contribute to the ongoing narrative of global gastronomy.

Navigating Culinary Challenges: When Surprises Turn Unconventional

While culinary journeys are often marked by delightful surprises, there are moments when unexpected finds take on a more challenging and unconventional character. In the markets of Southeast Asia, encounters with exotic ingredients such as durian and balut present an opportunity to confront personal culinary boundaries. The divisive nature of these items sparks a reflection on the subjectivity of taste and cultural perceptions of what is considered palatable.

Similarly, in the Nordic regions, the exploration of fermented delicacies such as surströmming—a pungent, fermented herring dish—pushes the boundaries of conventional flavor profiles. The initial shock gives way to an appreciation for the cultural significance of such preparations and a realization that culinary experiences, even when challenging, contribute to a broader understanding of global gastronomy.

Unconventional surprises underscore the diversity of global palates and the cultural contexts that shape culinary preferences. Navigating these challenges becomes an integral part of the culinary journey, prompting a deeper exploration of the intricacies that make each culinary tradition unique.

Conclusion: The Tapestry of Culinary Discoveries

In conclusion, the exploration of unexpected finds in global cuisine weaves a rich tapestry of culinary discoveries. From hidden street food gems to the revival of ancient traditions, each surprise adds a unique thread to the narrative of "Culinary Harmony." These moments of serendipity not only celebrate the diversity of global gastronomy but also invite readers to embrace the unexpected, to venture into the unknown, and to savor the delightful surprises that await on every culinary journey.

Chapter 2: Historical Evolution of Cuisines
Ancient Roots: Explore the ancient origins of global culinary traditions.

In the vast tapestry of global cuisine, the threads of tradition, flavor, and culinary innovation have been woven together over millennia. To truly understand the dishes that grace our tables today, we must embark on a journey back in time, tracing the ancient roots of culinary traditions that have shaped the way we eat and savor food. In "Culinary Harmony: Savoring Sustainable Gastronomy Across the Globe," the exploration of ancient culinary origins is a portal to the rich and diverse histories that underpin the world's gastronomic delights.

The Cradle of Civilization: Mesopotamia's Culinary Legacy

Our journey into the ancient roots of global cuisine begins in Mesopotamia, often regarded as the cradle of civilization. The fertile lands between the Tigris and Euphrates rivers were not only the birthplace of writing, mathematics, and governance but also the incubator of culinary traditions that would ripple through the ages.

In Mesopotamia, food was more than sustenance; it was an integral part of daily life and rituals. The region's ancient texts reveal a sophisticated understanding of ingredients, cooking techniques, and flavor combinations. Mesopotamian cooks were adept at using a diverse array of spices, herbs, and aromatic ingredients to enhance the flavors of their dishes. The clay tablets of cuneiform script unveil recipes for stews, bread, and barley-based dishes that showcase the culinary artistry of the time.

The advent of agriculture in Mesopotamia marked a pivotal moment in culinary history. The cultivation of grains, fruits, and vegetables allowed for the creation of diverse and nutritious meals. The Sumerians, one of the earliest civilizations in Mesopotamia, brewed beer, baked bread, and prepared elaborate feasts for religious ceremonies. The ancient Mesopotamians laid the foundations for culinary innovation, demonstrating a mastery of ingredients that would influence the cuisines of successive cultures.

From the Nile to the Mediterranean: Egyptian Culinary Traditions

The journey through ancient culinary origins takes us to the banks of the Nile, where the Egyptians cultivated a rich culinary heritage that left an indelible mark on global gastronomy. In ancient Egypt, food was not just sustenance; it was a reflection of the divine order, with certain foods believed to have spiritual significance.

Bread, a staple of the Egyptian diet, held a sacred status. The skill of baking and the variety of bread types reflected the culinary expertise of ancient Egyptian bakers. Hieroglyphs and wall paintings depict scenes of bread-making, beer brewing, and elaborate feasts, providing glimpses into the opulent culinary culture of the time.

The Nile River, a life-giving force, contributed to the abundance of ingredients available to the ancient Egyptians. Fish, grains, vegetables, and fruits were staples in their diet, and culinary practices such as drying, salting, and fermenting allowed for the preservation of food. The use of aromatic herbs and spices added depth and flavor to their dishes, with meals often accompanied by beer, a beverage held in high regard.

Egyptian culinary traditions extended beyond everyday meals to include lavish feasts associated with religious ceremonies and festivals. The preparation of offerings for the afterlife underscored the significance of food in Egyptian culture. The culinary legacy of ancient Egypt, with its emphasis on balance, symbolism, and a harmonious blend of flavors, set the stage for the development of Mediterranean cuisine.

The Spice Routes: Indic Influences on Culinary Diversity

As we continue our exploration of ancient culinary roots, the spice-laden winds of the Indian subcontinent beckon us to delve into the diverse and intricate flavors that emanated from this cultural epicenter. The ancient civilizations of India, China, and Southeast Asia played pivotal roles in shaping the culinary landscape of their regions and beyond.

In the Indian subcontinent, the Vedas, ancient sacred texts, offer insights into the early culinary practices of the region. Ayurveda, the ancient Indian system of medicine, emphasized the importance of balanced and nutritious meals, prescribing a harmonious combination of flavors to promote well-being. Spices such as black pepper, cardamom, and cinnamon found their way into the pots and pans of ancient Indian kitchens, creating a vibrant tapestry of flavors that continues to influence global cuisine.

The concept of curry, a term derived from the Tamil word "kari," was prevalent in ancient Indian cooking. The use of various spices, herbs, and locally available ingredients contributed to the diversity of curry preparations. Ancient Indian culinary traditions also embraced vegetarianism, with lentils, pulses, and vegetables taking center stage in many dishes.

The Silk Road, a network of trade routes connecting the East and West, became a conduit for the exchange of culinary ideas, ingredients, and techniques. Indian spices, including the coveted black pepper, cardamom, and ginger, traversed the Silk Road and left an indelible imprint on the cuisines of the Middle East and beyond.

The Birth of Gastronomy: Greece and the Mediterranean

Our exploration of ancient culinary origins would be incomplete without venturing into the sun-drenched landscapes of Greece and the Mediterranean, where the roots of gastronomy took hold, giving rise to a culinary legacy that continues to captivate the world.

Ancient Greece, with its emphasis on philosophy, arts, and the pursuit of knowledge, extended its intellectual curiosity to the realm of gastronomy. The writings of Archestratus, an ancient Greek poet and gastronome, provide glimpses into the culinary practices of the time. Archestratus celebrated the simplicity of fresh, seasonal ingredients and discouraged excessive use of spices, advocating for a purer and more natural expression of flavor.

The symposium, a convivial gathering of intellectuals, philosophers, and poets, became a platform for the enjoyment of food, wine, and intellectual discourse. The ancient Greeks elevated dining to an art form, emphasizing the importance of conviviality, moderation, and the appreciation of diverse flavors.

The influence of Greek gastronomy extended to the broader Mediterranean region, where culinary practices blended and evolved. Olive oil, a staple of ancient Greek cuisine, became a fundamental ingredient in Mediterranean cooking, shaping the distinct flavor profiles of dishes from Italy to Spain.

Rome: Culinary Conquests and Innovations

The culinary journey through ancient roots takes an imperial turn as we arrive in Rome, where culinary conquests and innovations marked the zenith of ancient gastronomy. The Romans, adept administrators and conquerors, assimilated culinary traditions from their vast empire, creating a culinary tapestry that reflected the diversity of their conquests.

Apicius, a Roman gourmet and author of the earliest known cookbook, "De Re Coquinaria" (On the Subject of Cooking), provides a window into the sophisticated culinary techniques of ancient Rome. The cookbook includes recipes that showcase a mastery of ingredients, cooking methods, and the use of exotic spices and herbs.

Roman cuisine embraced the concept of gustatio, or small appetizers, as a precursor to the main meal. The use of sauces, flavored oils, and herbs became integral to Roman cooking, adding layers of complexity to their dishes. The Romans also exhibited a keen interest in the theatricality of dining, with elaborate banquets featuring exotic ingredients and extravagant presentations.

The legacy of Roman gastronomy transcended the boundaries of the empire, influencing the culinary practices of regions under Roman rule. The adoption of ingredients such as olives, wine, and techniques like fermentation and pickling left an enduring impact on the development of European cuisines.

From the Silk Road to the Spice Islands: Asian Culinary Treasures

As we trace the ancient roots of global cuisine, the Spice Islands and the vast expanse of Asia beckon us with the promise of culinary treasures that have enriched the world's palates for centuries. The interplay of spices, flavors, and culinary techniques in Asia reveals a tapestry of gastronomic diversity that continues to captivate and inspire.

The Spice Islands, located in the Indonesian archipelago, were coveted for their precious cargo of spices such as cloves, nutmeg, and mace. These aromatic treasures, once a closely guarded secret, became the focus of maritime trade routes that connected the East to the West. The allure of these spices played a pivotal role in the age of exploration, shaping the destinies of nations and influencing the course of culinary history.

The culinary traditions of Southeast Asia, with their vibrant use of herbs, spices, and tropical ingredients, reflect the region's rich cultural tapestry. In Thailand, the balance of sweet, sour, salty, and spicy flavors creates a harmonious symphony in dishes like tom yum soup and green curry. The use of lemongrass, galangal, and kaffir lime leaves adds layers of complexity to Thai cuisine, embodying the essence of Southeast Asian culinary artistry.

The ancient roots of Chinese cuisine, deeply entwined with the philosophies of Confucianism and Taoism, reveal a reverence for balance, harmony, and the intrinsic qualities of ingredients. The art of stir-frying, steaming, and braising became integral to Chinese culinary techniques, allowing for the preservation of natural flavors and textures.

In India, the ancient roots of culinary traditions extend to the diverse regional cuisines that showcase a kaleidoscope of flavors. The use of spices, such as cumin, coriander, and cardamom, adds depth and complexity to dishes like biryani, curry, and masala chai. Ayurveda, the ancient Indian system of medicine, emphasizes the connection between food and well-being, influencing dietary practices that promote balance and holistic health.

The Culinary Legacy of the Americas: Aztec, Maya, and Inca

As we traverse the Atlantic Ocean, the ancient roots of global cuisine reveal the culinary legacies of the Americas—home to civilizations such as the Aztec, Maya, and Inca, whose agricultural innovations and culinary practices shaped the gastronomic landscape of the Western Hemisphere.

In the highlands of Mexico, the Aztecs cultivated a diverse array of crops, including maize (corn), beans, and squash. The combination of these staple ingredients, known as the "Three Sisters," formed the foundation of Aztec cuisine. Tortillas, a ubiquitous element of modern Mexican cuisine, trace their origins to the Aztecs, who perfected the art of nixtamalization to process maize.

The Aztecs also indulged in the consumption of chocolate, a beverage reserved for the elite. Flavored with vanilla and chili, the frothy concoction was enjoyed during religious ceremonies and as a symbol of wealth and luxury. The ancient roots of chocolate as a revered ingredient found in both sweet and savory preparations echo through the culinary traditions of Mexico and beyond.

In the Andean region of South America, the Inca civilization cultivated a remarkable variety of crops, including quinoa, potatoes, and maize. The Inca empire's agricultural innovations, such as terraced farming and crop diversification, laid the groundwork for sustaining large populations. Quinoa, once a staple of Incan diets, has experienced a revival in modern culinary trends, celebrated for its nutritional benefits and versatility.

The Maya civilization, nestled in the lush landscapes of Mesoamerica, embraced a diet centered around maize, beans, and cacao. The Maya's reverence for cacao extended beyond its use in beverages to include the creation of chocolate-based dishes, highlighting the ancient roots of chocolate's culinary prominence in the Americas.

The Silk Road and Culinary Fusion: Crossroads of Flavor

The ancient roots of global cuisine converge at the crossroads of the Silk Road, a historic network of trade routes that facilitated the exchange of goods, ideas, and culinary traditions between the East and West. As merchants traversed the Silk Road, they carried with them a caravan of flavors that would meld and evolve, giving rise to culinary fusion on an unprecedented scale.

In the Middle East, a cultural melting pot at the heart of the Silk Road, the convergence of culinary traditions created a tapestry of flavors that continue to define the region's gastronomy. The use of spices such as saffron, cinnamon, and cloves, combined with a mastery of techniques like slow-cooking and marinating, resulted in dishes like biryani, pilaf, and kebabs that showcase the richness of Middle Eastern culinary heritage.

In the Mediterranean, where the Silk Road connected East to West, the exchange of ingredients and culinary techniques became a catalyst for gastronomic innovation. The incorporation of spices from the East, such as pepper and cinnamon, into Mediterranean cuisines added a layer of complexity to dishes like paella, couscous, and tagines. The blending of flavors from diverse cultures along the Silk Road created a harmonious fusion that transcended geographical boundaries.

Conclusion: The Culinary Odyssey Through Time

In conclusion, the exploration of ancient roots in global cuisine unfolds as a captivating odyssey through time, tracing the culinary legacies of civilizations that have shaped the way we eat and savor food. From the fertile plains of Mesopotamia to the spice-laden markets of Asia, from the sun-drenched landscapes of Greece to the culinary conquests of Rome, and from the ancient traditions of the Americas to the crossroads of the Silk Road, the journey through culinary history is a testament to the resilience, innovation, and interconnectedness of human cultures.

The ancient roots of global cuisine provide a foundation upon which modern gastronomy stands, a legacy that continues to evolve and adapt to the changing tastes and preferences of a globalized world. As we savor the diverse flavors on our plates today, we pay homage to the culinary pioneers of antiquity whose innovations and traditions have woven a rich tapestry of global gastronomy—a tapestry that continues to unfold, inviting us to embark on new culinary journeys and savor the timeless connection between food, culture, and history.

Trade Routes Influence: Discuss the impact of historical trade routes.

In the annals of culinary history, the influence of trade routes stands as a testament to the interconnectedness of cultures through the exchange of goods, ideas, and, perhaps most notably, spices. As caravans traversed deserts, ships sailed vast oceans, and merchants bartered along ancient routes, they not only facilitated commerce but also created a culinary kaleidoscope, blending flavors from distant lands and shaping the course of global gastronomy.

Silk Road: A Tapestry of Flavors

The Silk Road, a network of interconnected trade routes that spanned Asia, the Middle East, and parts of Europe, was not only a conduit for silk, spices, and precious goods but also a highway for culinary cross-pollination. This ancient thoroughfare facilitated the exchange of culinary traditions, ingredients, and techniques that would leave an indelible mark on the cuisines of the regions it connected.

Spices, often referred to as the "gold of the East," were among the most coveted commodities traded along the Silk Road. Cinnamon, cloves, ginger, and pepper, sourced from the exotic landscapes of Southeast Asia and the Indian subcontinent, found their way westward, transforming the palates of the Middle East and Europe. In return, the East welcomed new ingredients such as grapes, olives, and figs, introduced via the same trade routes.

As merchants and traders moved along the Silk Road, they not only exchanged goods but also shared culinary practices. The Middle Eastern love for spices, evident in dishes like biryani and kebabs, reflects the influence of Eastern flavors. Conversely, the East embraced the use of

Mediterranean ingredients, contributing to the creation of dishes like curries infused with a hint of European herbs.

The Silk Road not only enriched the spice cabinets of nations but also fostered a spirit of cultural curiosity that transcended borders. Culinary techniques, cooking methods, and the art of flavor combinations became part of a shared heritage that resonates in the kitchens of diverse cultures even today.

Spice Islands: A Culinary Treasure Trove

The Spice Islands, also known as the Moluccas or Maluku Islands in Indonesia, emerged as a focal point in the global spice trade during the Age of Exploration. These islands were the exclusive source of coveted spices such as cloves, nutmeg, and mace, making them valuable commodities that fueled maritime expeditions and sparked geopolitical intrigue.

European powers, including Portugal, Spain, the Netherlands, and later, England, sought control over the Spice Islands to gain a monopoly on these precious spices. The race to dominate the spice trade led to exploratory voyages, naval battles, and the establishment of trade routes that would reshape global culinary landscapes.

The impact of Spice Islands' spices on European cuisine was transformative. The addition of cloves, nutmeg, and cinnamon not only enhanced the flavor profiles of dishes but also played a role in preserving food in an era before refrigeration. Spice-laden recipes became status symbols, showcasing the wealth and sophistication of those who could afford these exotic ingredients.

Culinary fusion flourished as the Spice Islands' treasures influenced both sweet and savory European dishes. Spiced cakes, pies, and mulled beverages became popular, incorporating the aromatic richness of the East into European culinary traditions. The global exchange of flavors, facilitated by the Spice Islands, laid the groundwork for a culinary tapestry that would continue to evolve through the centuries.

Impact on Mediterranean Cuisine: A Fusion of East and West

The Mediterranean, with its diverse array of cultures and climates, became a melting pot of culinary influences thanks to the interconnectedness facilitated by trade routes. The convergence of Eastern and Western flavors along the Mediterranean Sea created a region of culinary innovation and gastronomic excellence.

Trade routes connecting the Mediterranean with the Middle East introduced a plethora of ingredients and spices to the cuisines of Greece, Rome, and beyond. The use of cinnamon, cumin, and coriander in Mediterranean dishes reflects the enduring impact of these trade interactions. The spice trade also contributed to the popularity of wine, as the addition of aromatic spices and herbs transformed ordinary wines into spiced elixirs enjoyed by the elite.

The Arab influence on Mediterranean cuisine, facilitated by trade routes across the sea, brought new techniques and ingredients to the region. The use of rice, citrus fruits, and almonds in dishes like paella and tagines bears witness to this cross-cultural exchange. The art of preserving lemons, a staple in many Middle Eastern and Mediterranean dishes, showcases the practical adaptations that emerged from trade routes.

Additionally, the introduction of new cooking methods, such as grilling and marinating, added depth and complexity to Mediterranean cuisine. Spices like saffron and sumac, acquired through trade, became integral to the flavor profiles of iconic dishes like paella and kebabs. The fusion of East and West along Mediterranean trade routes gave rise to a culinary landscape that embraced diversity, innovation, and a celebration of flavors.

Influences on Asian Cuisines: Spice Routes and Culinary Fusion

Asia, with its vast expanse and diverse cultures, witnessed the convergence of culinary traditions along ancient spice routes. The maritime spice trade that connected Southeast Asia, India, China, and the Middle East not only shaped the flavors of individual cuisines but also fostered a spirit of culinary fusion that transcended national borders.

The Silk Road, extending into Central Asia and the Indian subcontinent, brought spices from the East to regions that would later become known for their culinary diversity. Indian spices, in particular, became integral to the culinary traditions of Southeast Asia, as traders and settlers carried the flavors of cumin, coriander, and cardamom across maritime routes.

In the Indian subcontinent, the impact of spice routes is evident in the diverse regional cuisines. Coastal regions embraced the abundance of seafood and incorporated spices like black pepper, cloves, and cinnamon into their culinary repertoire. Inland regions showcased the versatility of spices in dishes like biryani and kebabs, reflecting the historical trade connections with the Middle East and Central Asia.

Trade routes also played a pivotal role in the spread of tea culture across Asia. The ancient tea trade routes, connecting China with Tibet, Mongolia, and later, Europe, facilitated the exchange of tea leaves and tea culture. The tea trade not only influenced regional variations in tea preparation but also led to the creation of new tea blends, such as chai in India and jasmine tea in China.

Influence on European Culinary Renaissance: The Spice Renaissance

The Renaissance in Europe, spanning the 14th to the 17th centuries, marked a period of profound cultural, artistic, and intellectual revival. As trade routes expanded and explorers ventured into new territories, the culinary world experienced a renaissance of its own, driven by the influx of exotic ingredients and spices from distant lands.

The Spice Renaissance, as it is often called, transformed European cuisine by introducing a myriad of flavors previously unknown to Western palates. Spices such as black pepper, cinnamon, and ginger became highly sought after and were considered symbols of wealth and prestige. The culinary landscape of European courts and aristocratic households was forever changed as exotic spices found their way into recipes, giving rise to a culinary opulence that celebrated the abundance of the spice trade.

The use of spices in European cuisine during the Renaissance extended beyond flavor enhancement to include medicinal and preservative properties. Spices were believed to have health benefits, and their use in preserving meats and other perishables became crucial in an era before refrigeration. This dual role of spices as both flavor enhancers and practical kitchen aids contributed to their widespread adoption in European kitchens.

As the culinary arts flourished during the Renaissance, cookbooks and culinary manuscripts began to document the creative use of spices in European cuisine. Recipes for spiced wines, elaborate meat dishes, and sweet treats adorned with exotic flavors became popular among the elite. The culinary techniques and flavor combinations introduced during the Spice Renaissance laid the foundation for the diverse and sophisticated European cuisines we know today.

Colonial Trade Routes: The Global Culinary Exchange

The Age of Exploration and colonial expansion opened new chapters in the culinary history of the world. As European powers established colonies in the Americas, Africa, and Asia, they not only sought wealth in the form of spices, precious metals, and agricultural commodities but also engaged in a global culinary exchange that would redefine diets on both sides of the Atlantic.

The Columbian Exchange, named after Christopher Columbus, initiated the transfer of plants, animals, and culinary traditions between the Old World and the New World. While this exchange had profound ecological and economic implications, it also led to a fusion of flavors that forever altered the culinary landscapes of Europe, Africa, and the Americas.

The introduction of New World ingredients to the Old World had a profound impact on European cuisine. Staples like tomatoes, potatoes, corn, and chili peppers became integral to European diets, revolutionizing culinary practices. The potato, in particular, emerged as a versatile and essential ingredient in European cooking, contributing to the development of dishes such as mashed potatoes and gnocchi.

The global trade routes established during the colonial era also shaped the culinary heritage of regions like Southeast Asia and the Caribbean. The exchange of ingredients such as coconut, pineapple, and cassava between Africa, Asia, and the Americas created a fusion of flavors that defines the vibrant cuisines of these regions.

Conclusion: Culinary Legacy of Trade Routes

In conclusion, the impact of historical trade routes on the evolution of cuisines is a saga of culinary fusion, innovation, and shared heritage. From the Silk Road's tapestry of flavors to the Spice Islands' treasure trove, from the Mediterranean's cross-cultural exchange to the global culinary exchange of the colonial era, trade routes have shaped the way we eat, cook, and savor food.

The interconnectedness fostered by trade routes has left an indelible mark on the culinary map, transcending geographic boundaries and cultural differences. The exchange of ingredients, techniques, and culinary traditions has given rise to a global pantry that reflects the diversity and richness of human history.

As we explore the impact of trade routes on the historical evolution of cuisines, we embark on a culinary journey that echoes the footsteps of traders, merchants, and explorers who traversed the world in pursuit of spices, treasures, and the shared experience of breaking bread together. The legacy of trade routes lives on in our kitchens, where the fusion of flavors continues to celebrate the interwoven stories of cultures brought together by the universal language of food.

Culinary Revolutions: Highlight historical events catalyzing culinary transformations.

In the grand tapestry of culinary history, certain epochs stand out as pivotal moments that catalyzed profound transformations in the way people approached food, cooking, and dining. Culinary revolutions, often spurred by a confluence of cultural, social, and technological factors, have left an indelible mark on global cuisines, shaping the way we perceive, prepare, and enjoy food.

The Agricultural Revolution: Nourishing the Dawn of Civilization

At the dawn of human civilization, the transition from nomadic hunter-gatherer lifestyles to settled agricultural communities marked a revolutionary shift in the way people sourced, cultivated, and consumed food. The Agricultural Revolution, spanning several millennia, laid the foundation for the development of complex societies and the diversification of culinary practices.

The cultivation of crops such as wheat, barley, rice, and legumes brought about a surplus of food that supported larger populations. As communities embraced agriculture, a culinary evolution unfolded, with the advent of baking, fermentation, and other transformative cooking techniques. Grains gave rise to bread, a staple that transcended cultures and became a symbol of sustenance and community.

The Agricultural Revolution also witnessed the domestication of animals, contributing to the emergence of diverse culinary traditions centered around meat-based dishes. The cultivation of fruits and vegetables further enriched the culinary landscape, fostering creativity in flavor combinations and culinary techniques.

Feasts of Antiquity: Culinary Extravagance in Ancient Civilizations

The great civilizations of antiquity, including Mesopotamia, Egypt, Greece, and Rome, elevated feasting to an art form that reflected social hierarchies, religious beliefs, and cultural values. Culinary extravagance during festivals, banquets, and religious ceremonies became a means of expressing opulence, power, and communal identity.

In Mesopotamia, the Epic of Gilgamesh recounts lavish feasts where kings and nobles indulged in a variety of dishes and drinks. The culinary prowess of Mesopotamian chefs extended to the preparation of sumptuous stews, flatbreads, and desserts, showcasing the sophistication of ancient culinary arts.

In ancient Egypt, banquets held in honor of gods and pharaohs featured a diverse array of dishes, including bread, beer, honey, and meats. The symbolic significance of certain foods, such as bread and beer representing life and sustenance, underscored the spiritual dimension of Egyptian feasting.

The symposiums of ancient Greece became legendary for their combination of intellectual discourse and indulgent dining. Greek philosophers, including Plato and Aristotle, pondered life's complexities while partaking in elaborate banquets featuring wine, fruits, and a variety of meat dishes.

Ancient Rome, with its grand feasts and culinary excesses, showcased the culinary innovations of the time. Apicius, a renowned Roman gastronome, left behind a cookbook that documented recipes for intricate dishes, revealing the diverse ingredients and cooking techniques employed in ancient Roman kitchens.

These feasts of antiquity not only exemplified culinary artistry but also played a role in shaping cultural norms, social rituals, and the perception of food as a medium for both sustenance and cultural expression.

The Spice Routes and Culinary Exploration: A Culinary Renaissance

The Age of Exploration, spanning the 15th to the 17th centuries, ushered in an era of culinary renaissance as maritime trade routes connected the Old World with the riches of the East. The quest for spices, exotic ingredients, and new culinary experiences fueled a fervor for exploration that transcended geographical boundaries.

European powers, including Portugal, Spain, the Netherlands, and England, embarked on ambitious voyages in search of direct sea routes to Asia. The spice trade, centered around the coveted spices of the East such as pepper, cinnamon, and nutmeg, became a driving force behind these explorations.

The culinary impact of the Spice Routes was profound. The introduction of new spices and ingredients revolutionized European cuisine, leading to a shift in flavor profiles and cooking techniques. Spices were no longer rare commodities reserved for the elite; they permeated kitchens across Europe, transforming the way food was seasoned, preserved, and enjoyed.

The Spice Routes not only enriched European cuisines but also sparked culinary curiosity and innovation. The blending of East and West, as seen in dishes like spiced stews, curries, and pastries, exemplified a fusion of flavors that transcended cultural boundaries. The culinary renaissance triggered by the Spice Routes laid the groundwork for the diverse and globalized cuisines we savor today.

The Culinary Legacy of the French Revolution: Haute Cuisine Emerges

The French Revolution, a tumultuous period of political and social upheaval in the late 18th century, had a profound impact on the culinary landscape of France and, by extension, the world. As the revolutionary fervor swept through the nation, it also touched the kitchens of aristocratic households, leading to the emergence of a new culinary era known as Haute Cuisine.

The dismantling of the French monarchy and the rise of revolutionary ideals ushered in a spirit of egalitarianism that extended to the culinary realm. The elaborate and decadent feasts of the aristocracy gave way to a more refined and sophisticated approach to cooking. Chefs, who had previously served noble households, found themselves adapting to the changing political landscape by embracing simplicity, precision, and artistic presentation.

One of the central figures in this culinary revolution was Marie-Antoine Carême, a chef and pâtissier who is often regarded as the founder of Haute Cuisine. Carême's culinary innovations included the development of intricate sauces, elaborate pastry creations, and a meticulous approach to food presentation. His emphasis on technique, aesthetics, and the use of quality ingredients became hallmarks of Haute Cuisine.

The culinary legacy of the French Revolution extended beyond France, influencing culinary practices across Europe and beyond. The principles of Haute Cuisine, with its emphasis on culinary artistry and meticulous preparation, laid the foundation for modern gastronomy and elevated cooking to an art form.

Industrialization and the Birth of Convenience Foods: A Culinary Paradigm Shift

The advent of the Industrial Revolution in the 19th century brought about transformative changes in various aspects of society, including the way food was produced, distributed, and consumed. The shift from agrarian economies to industrialized urban centers led to a reimagining of culinary practices and the birth of convenience foods.

Industrialization brought innovations such as canning, pasteurization, and refrigeration, which revolutionized food preservation and distribution. Canned goods, preserved meats, and condensed soups became staples in households, offering unprecedented convenience and extended shelf life. This marked a departure from traditional cooking methods that relied on fresh, locally sourced ingredients.

The rise of convenience foods was further fueled by advancements in food processing and packaging. Companies like Campbell's, Nestlé, and Heinz introduced a range of processed foods, from canned soups to condensed milk, that appealed to the busy lifestyles of urban dwellers. These innovations not only saved time in the kitchen but also contributed to the standardization of flavors and the global availability of certain food products.

The culinary landscape shifted as home cooks embraced the ease of incorporating pre-packaged and processed foods into their meals. Convenience became a defining factor in food choices, and the concept of quick and easy meals became embedded in modern culinary culture. While convenience foods offered efficiency, they also raised questions about nutritional value, flavor authenticity, and the impact on traditional culinary skills.

Fast Food Revolution: The Globalization of Quick Service Dining

The latter half of the 20th century witnessed the rise of the fast-food industry, marking a revolution in the way people approached dining and food consumption. The globalization of fast-food chains, such as McDonald's, KFC, and Pizza Hut, transformed the culinary landscape by introducing standardized menus, rapid service, and a new paradigm of convenience dining.

Rooted in the principles of efficiency, affordability, and consistency, fast food became a ubiquitous presence in urban centers worldwide. The appeal of quick-service dining extended beyond the food itself; it embodied a lifestyle characterized by speed, convenience, and accessibility. The standardization of menus and recipes allowed fast-food chains to offer familiar experiences to customers, regardless of their location.

The globalization of fast food had profound cultural implications, influencing dietary habits, culinary preferences, and even perceptions of leisure and socializing. The fast-food revolution also sparked debates about health, sustainability, and the impact of mass-produced, processed foods on public well-being.

While fast food introduced unparalleled convenience and accessibility, it also prompted a reevaluation of culinary values. The rise of the slow food movement, advocating for the preservation of traditional cooking methods, local ingredients, and mindful dining, emerged as a counterpoint to the fast-food phenomenon. The tension between fast food and slow food reflected broader discussions about the role of food in society, the consequences of mass production, and the importance of culinary heritage.

Technological Advancements and Molecular Gastronomy: A Culinary Frontier

The turn of the 21st century brought about a new frontier in culinary exploration with the advent of molecular gastronomy. This culinary movement, characterized by the application of scientific principles and innovative techniques to food preparation, challenged traditional notions of cooking and presentation.

Pioneered by chefs like Ferran Adrià of elBulli in Spain and Heston Blumenthal of The Fat Duck in the UK, molecular gastronomy introduced unconventional methods such as spherification, foaming, and the use of liquid nitrogen. These techniques allowed chefs to manipulate the physical and chemical properties of ingredients, creating avant-garde dishes that pushed the boundaries of culinary creativity.

The incorporation of scientific principles into the culinary arts brought about a reimagining of textures, flavors, and presentations. Foam-filled spheres, edible films, and frozen powders became staples of molecular gastronomy, challenging diners to rethink their expectations of what constitutes a meal.

Technological advancements in the culinary sphere extended beyond molecular gastronomy. The rise of digital technology and social media transformed the way people engage with food, from sharing recipes and restaurant experiences online to accessing virtual cooking classes and food delivery services. The intersection of technology and food opened up new possibilities for culinary exploration and community engagement.

Conclusion: The Culinary Tapestry of Evolution

In conclusion, the historical evolution of cuisines is a dynamic tapestry woven with threads of agricultural ingenuity, cultural feasts, spice-laden exploration, revolutions in gastronomy, industrialization's convenience, fast food's global impact, and the technological frontiers of molecular gastronomy. Each chapter in this culinary saga represents a revolution that has shaped the way we grow, prepare, and savor food.

These culinary revolutions not only reflect the resilience and adaptability of human societies but also highlight the intrinsic connection between food and the cultural, social, and technological landscapes of their times. As we navigate the diverse culinary landscapes of today, we find ourselves standing on the shoulders of those who, throughout history, have reshaped the world on our plates. The ongoing evolution of cuisines is a testament to the ever-changing nature of human tastes, preferences, and culinary creativity—a journey that continues to unfold with every shared meal and each new culinary discovery.

Migration's Culinary Impact: Explore how migration shapes global cuisine diversity.

In the vast and intricate mosaic of global cuisines, the influence of migration emerges as a central thread, weaving together flavors, techniques, and traditions from diverse corners of the world. As people migrated across continents and oceans, they carried with them not only their belongings but also their culinary heritage, enriching and transforming the gastronomic landscapes they encountered. The interplay between migration and cuisine is a captivating tale of adaptation, fusion, and the continual evolution of flavors.

Ancient Migrations: The Cradle of Culinary Diversity

From the earliest human migrations out of Africa to the spread of Homo sapiens across Europe and Asia, ancient populations traversed landscapes, adapting to new environments, and exchanging culinary knowledge. The movement of ancient nomadic tribes and early settlers laid the groundwork for the diverse culinary tapestry we witness today.

The Silk Road, an ancient network of trade routes connecting East and West, facilitated not only the exchange of goods but also the mingling of culinary traditions. As merchants and travelers journeyed along this vast web of interconnected routes, they brought with them spices, herbs, and cooking techniques that left an indelible mark on the cuisines of the regions they touched.

Similarly, the movement of people within the Mediterranean basin—Phoenicians, Greeks, Romans—contributed to the amalgamation of culinary practices. Olive oil, grapes, and wheat, essential elements of Mediterranean cuisine, spread as people migrated and established new communities, influencing the diets of diverse cultures.

Culinary Crossroads: The Impact of Migration in Asia

Asia, with its vast expanse and rich cultural diversity, bears witness to the profound impact of migration on culinary traditions. The Silk Road, extending into Central Asia and the Indian subcontinent, became a melting pot where flavors and ingredients from East and West converged.

The migration of the Mongols, for instance, brought dairy-centric dishes like yogurt and kefir to regions where they were not traditionally consumed. The nomadic lifestyle of the Mongols necessitated portable and easily preserved food, influencing the development of dishes that could withstand the rigors of travel.

In Southeast Asia, the movement of populations across maritime routes shaped the region's culinary identity. The Austronesian migration, for example, contributed to the spread of ingredients like coconuts, taro, and sweet potatoes across the Pacific Islands, fostering a shared culinary heritage among island communities.

The Columbian Exchange: Culinary Fusion in the Americas

The Age of Exploration, marked by Christopher Columbus's voyages to the Americas, initiated a monumental exchange of flora, fauna, and culinary traditions between the Old World and the New World. The Columbian Exchange, while transforming global agriculture, also had a profound impact on the culinary landscapes of Europe, Africa, and the Americas.

New World ingredients such as tomatoes, potatoes, corn, and chili peppers made their way to Europe, becoming integral components of European cuisines. The humble potato, in particular, reshaped diets by providing a versatile and reliable source of sustenance, eventually leading to the creation of dishes like French fries and mashed potatoes.

In the Americas, the introduction of Old World ingredients like wheat, rice, and livestock transformed indigenous culinary practices. The fusion of Old and New World ingredients gave rise to innovative dishes such as corned beef and cabbage in the Americas, reflecting the intersection of culinary traditions from both sides of the Atlantic.

Diaspora and Culinary Hybridization: A Taste of Global Migration

The forced migration of African communities during the transatlantic slave trade profoundly influenced the culinary landscape of the Americas. African culinary traditions, rich in spices, grains, and root vegetables, melded with Indigenous and European ingredients, creating a unique fusion of flavors that persists in dishes like gumbo, jambalaya, and collard greens.

Similarly, the Chinese diaspora played a pivotal role in the spread of Chinese culinary traditions across the globe. Chinese immigrants, particularly in Southeast Asia and the Americas, adapted their traditional recipes to local ingredients and preferences, giving rise to distinctive regional variations of Chinese cuisine.

The Jewish diaspora, marked by centuries of migration and dispersion, contributed to the global diversity of Jewish cuisine. From the bagels of Eastern Europe to the Sephardic dishes of the Mediterranean, Jewish culinary traditions evolved in response to the cultural landscapes of the communities in which they settled.

Colonial Migrations: A Culinary Legacy Across Continents

The colonial era, with its waves of exploration and migration, left an enduring imprint on global cuisines. European powers established colonies in the Americas, Africa, and Asia, introducing new ingredients and culinary techniques that merged with existing local traditions.

The fusion of European, African, and Indigenous cuisines in the Americas gave rise to a multitude of dishes that define the culinary landscapes of countries like Brazil, Mexico, and the United States. Ingredients such as maize, beans, tomatoes, and chili peppers became staples, forming the foundation of dishes like tortillas, casseroles, and salsas.

In Africa, the impact of colonialism on culinary traditions is evident in the fusion of indigenous ingredients with European imports. The introduction of crops like maize, cassava, and peanuts transformed African diets, leading to the creation of dishes such as fufu, couscous, and groundnut stew.

In Asia, colonial migrations influenced the blending of culinary traditions. The British, for instance, introduced tea and spices to India, contributing to the rich tapestry of Indian cuisine. Similarly, the Dutch brought Indonesian culinary influences to the Netherlands, resulting in the popularization of dishes like nasi goreng.

Modern Migrations: Diversity on the Global Table

In the modern era, globalization, increased connectivity, and mass migrations have further shaped the diversity of global cuisines. The movement of people across borders, whether for economic, political, or social reasons, has led to the exchange of culinary practices and the integration of diverse flavors into local food scenes.

Urbanization and the rise of multicultural societies have given birth to culinary hubs where people from different cultural backgrounds share their culinary heritage. Cities like New York, London, and Sydney boast vibrant food scenes that reflect the diversity of their populations, offering a kaleidoscope of flavors from around the world.

The fusion of culinary traditions in modern migrations is exemplified by the phenomenon of "fusion cuisine," where chefs and home cooks experiment with blending flavors and techniques from different culinary backgrounds. Dishes that seamlessly combine elements from various traditions have become emblematic of the globalized nature of contemporary cuisine.

Conclusion: A Global Banquet of Migration and Flavor

In conclusion, the interplay between migration and cuisine has been a driving force in the evolution of global culinary diversity. From ancient nomads traversing the Silk Road to the forced migrations of the transatlantic slave trade, and from the colonial exchange of ingredients to the modern fusion of culinary traditions, migration has left an indelible mark on what we eat and how we eat it.

As we savor the diverse flavors on our plates, we partake in a global banquet that bears witness to the journeys of countless individuals and communities across time and space. The culinary impact of migration is not only a testament to human adaptability but also a celebration of the rich tapestry of cultures that have come together, each contributing a unique ingredient to the global feast of flavors.

Chapter 3: Iconic Dishes
Cultural Cornerstones: Explore iconic dishes symbolizing cultural heritage and excellence.

In the vast and diverse landscape of global cuisines, certain dishes rise above the rest, not just in terms of flavor but as symbols of cultural identity and culinary excellence. These iconic dishes serve as cultural cornerstones, embodying the rich heritage, traditions, and artistry of their respective communities. As we embark on a journey through these culinary masterpieces, we discover the stories, rituals, and flavors that make them enduring symbols of cultural pride.

Sushi: Japanese Elegance on a Plate

No exploration of iconic dishes is complete without delving into the world of sushi, a culinary art form that epitomizes Japanese elegance and precision. Sushi, with its origins in the Edo period, has evolved into a global sensation, celebrated for its harmonious blend of flavors, textures, and visual appeal.

At the heart of sushi lies the art of rice preparation, where each grain is seasoned with a delicate balance of rice vinegar, sugar, and salt. This seasoned rice becomes the canvas for an array of ingredients, from fresh sashimi-grade fish to vegetables and seaweed. The meticulous art of sushi making, known as "shokunin," requires years of apprenticeship to master the techniques of slicing, rolling, and presenting each piece.

The cultural significance of sushi extends beyond its delectable taste. It reflects the Japanese reverence for nature, seen in the emphasis on seasonality and the use of fresh, local ingredients. The act of enjoying sushi becomes a ritual, a sensory experience that encompasses taste, sight, and touch.

Whether enjoyed at a humble street vendor or an exclusive sushi bar, each bite of sushi tells a story of craftsmanship and cultural pride.

Pizza Napoletana: A Slice of Italian Tradition

From the streets of Naples to pizzerias around the world, Pizza Napoletana stands as a testament to the simplicity and brilliance of Italian culinary tradition. This iconic dish, with its thin, chewy crust, vibrant tomato sauce, fresh mozzarella, and a touch of basil, has become a global favorite, transcending cultural boundaries and inspiring countless variations.

The story of Pizza Napoletana is deeply intertwined with the history of Naples, where it originated in the 18th century. The dish was initially a humble street food, sold by vendors who used local ingredients to create an affordable and delicious meal for the working class. Over the years, it evolved into a symbol of Neapolitan culinary pride.

The production of authentic Pizza Napoletana is guided by strict standards. The dough must be made with specific types of flour, water, salt, and yeast, and it must undergo a slow fermentation process. The tomatoes used in the sauce are often San Marzano tomatoes, prized for their sweetness and low acidity. The cheese, typically mozzarella di bufala, adds a creamy richness to the final creation.

This culinary masterpiece has earned recognition beyond Italy, with the Associazione Vera Pizza Napoletana (AVPN) certifying pizzerias worldwide that adhere to the authentic Neapolitan pizza-making tradition. Each slice of Pizza Napoletana carries not just the flavors of Italy but the spirit of a city and its people.

Biryani: The Fragrant Jewel of South Asia

Biryani, a dish that marries aromatic rice with flavorful meats and spices, stands as a fragrant jewel in the culinary crown of South Asia. This iconic dish, with its roots in the royal kitchens of the Mughal Empire, has evolved into a symbol of celebration, community, and culinary artistry across the Indian subcontinent.

At its core, biryani is a celebration of rice—a canvas that absorbs the essence of aromatic spices, herbs, and proteins. The layers of rice and meat, slow-cooked to perfection, create a symphony of flavors and textures. The variations of biryani are as diverse as the regions it hails from, each with its unique blend of spices and techniques.

The cultural significance of biryani extends to festive occasions, family gatherings, and communal feasts. It is a dish that transcends religious and cultural divides, embraced by Hindus, Muslims, and others alike. The meticulous preparation of biryani involves marinating the meat, parboiling the rice, and layering the two with a medley of spices. The final touch is the "dum" cooking technique, where the biryani is slow-cooked in a sealed pot, allowing the flavors to meld.

Biryani's journey from the royal courts to the bustling streets reflects the resilience and adaptability of South Asian culinary traditions. Whether enjoyed in the opulence of a banquet or savored at a roadside eatery, biryani remains a testament to the art of flavor alchemy that defines the region's rich culinary heritage.

Croissant: Layers of French Mastery

In the realm of French pastries, the croissant stands as a pinnacle of culinary mastery, its flaky layers and buttery richness capturing the essence of French indulgence. This iconic viennoiserie, with its crescent shape and golden exterior, has become synonymous with French breakfast culture and refined patisserie.

The origins of the croissant can be traced back to Austria, but its transformation into the delicate, laminated pastry we know today is a testament to French ingenuity. The process of creating croissants involves layering butter between layers of dough, a technique known as laminating. This meticulous process results in the distinct flakiness and rich flavor that define the croissant.

The cultural significance of the croissant in France goes beyond its delectable taste. It has become a symbol of joie de vivre, often enjoyed leisurely with a cup of coffee in a Parisian cafe. The ritual of biting into a freshly baked croissant, with its delicate crunch and tender interior, is a sensory experience that embodies the French art of savoring life's simple pleasures.

While the classic croissant remains a timeless favorite, French pastry chefs continually innovate, introducing variations such as almond croissants, pain au chocolat, and savory twists. The croissant's journey from the historic Viennese kipferl to the refined French patisserie reflects the dynamic nature of culinary evolution and the global appeal of French baking traditions.

Tacos: Mexico's Culinary Ambassadors

In the vibrant tapestry of Mexican cuisine, tacos emerge as culinary ambassadors, representing the diversity, bold flavors, and communal spirit of this rich culinary tradition. From street vendors to high-end restaurants, tacos have become synonymous with Mexican gastronomy, transcending borders and winning the hearts of food enthusiasts worldwide.

At its core, a taco is a simple creation—an assembly of a tortilla and a filling. Yet, within this simplicity lies a world of variety. Tacos can feature an array of fillings, from grilled meats like carne asada and al pastor to seafood, vegetables, and slow-cooked stews. The choice of toppings, salsas, and garnishes adds layers of complexity and depth to the taco experience.

The cultural significance of tacos in Mexico goes beyond their culinary appeal. Tacos are a social food, often enjoyed in the company of friends and family. The taco stand, or taquería, is a communal space where people gather to savor these handheld delights. The act of crafting a taco—choosing the tortilla, adding the filling, and selecting the toppings—is an interactive experience that reflects the diversity of Mexican regional cuisines.

Tacos have become global ambassadors of Mexican culinary heritage, with variations and interpretations found in cities around the world. The street food culture and the art of taco-making have inspired chefs and home cooks alike to experiment with flavors and techniques, creating a global fusion that pays homage to the authenticity and vibrancy of Mexican tacos.

Conclusion: Icons on the Global Plate

In conclusion, these iconic dishes—sushi, Pizza Napoletana, biryani, croissants, and tacos—transcend their culinary origins to become symbols of cultural pride, culinary excellence, and shared human experiences. Each dish tells a story of innovation, tradition, and the profound connection between food and culture. As we savor these iconic creations, we partake in a global feast that celebrates the diversity and richness of the human culinary journey.

Chef Legends: Introduce chefs influencing iconic dish creation and popularity.

In the realm of gastronomy, behind every iconic dish lies the vision, skill, and creativity of a master chef. These culinary virtuosos, often referred to as chef legends, shape the landscape of global cuisine through their innovative techniques, dedication to quality, and a passion for pushing the boundaries of flavor. In this exploration of iconic dishes, we delve into the stories of the chefs who have left an indelible mark on culinary history, elevating simple ingredients into legendary creations.

Jiro Ono: The Sushi Maestro

When it comes to the art of sushi, one name stands out as a true maestro—Jiro Ono. The octogenarian chef, based in Tokyo, has devoted his life to perfecting the craft of sushi-making, earning him the title of "sushi god" and global recognition. Jiro's sushi restaurant, Sukiyabashi Jiro, is a tiny, unassuming establishment in the upscale district of Ginza, yet it holds three Michelin stars and is considered one of the world's best sushi restaurants.

Jiro's approach to sushi is deeply traditional, rooted in the principles of Edomae-zushi, a style that originated in the Edo period. He insists on using the freshest, highest-quality ingredients, sourcing fish directly from Tokyo's Tsukiji Fish Market. The rice, a crucial element of sushi, is seasoned with a delicate touch, allowing the natural flavors of the fish to shine.

Beyond his technical mastery, Jiro embodies the discipline and dedication characteristic of a true chef legend. His rigorous training regimen, attention to detail, and pursuit of perfection have inspired a generation of chefs. The documentary "Jiro Dreams of Sushi" provides a glimpse into the life and philosophy of this culinary icon, revealing the sacrifices and passion that define his approach to sushi.

Julia Child: The French Cooking Pioneer

In the realm of French cuisine, Julia Child stands as an iconic figure who introduced the art of French cooking to American households. Born in Pasadena, California, Julia embarked on a culinary journey that would reshape the landscape of home cooking and popularize French techniques in the United States.

Julia's groundbreaking television series, "The French Chef," made its debut in 1963, bringing her affable personality and infectious enthusiasm to viewers across the nation. With her distinctive voice and unpretentious approach, Julia demystified French cooking, making it accessible to a wide audience. Her iconic cookbook, "Mastering the Art of French Cooking," co-authored with Simone Beck and Louisette Bertholle, became a culinary bible for aspiring home cooks.

One of Julia's signature dishes, coq au vin, exemplifies her commitment to authentic French flavors and techniques. The slow-cooked dish, featuring chicken braised in red wine with mushrooms, bacon, and onions, showcases the depth and richness of classical French cuisine. Julia's influence extends beyond recipes; she instilled in her audience a love for culinary exploration and the joy of savoring well-prepared meals.

Massimo Bottura: The Modern Italian Innovator

In the contemporary culinary landscape, Massimo Bottura stands as a visionary chef who has redefined the boundaries of Italian cuisine. Born and raised in Modena, Italy, Bottura is the creative force behind Osteria Francescana, a three-Michelin-starred restaurant consistently ranked among the world's best.

Bottura's approach to Italian cuisine is marked by innovation, artistic presentation, and a deep respect for tradition. His iconic dish, "Oops! I Dropped the Lemon Tart," is a playful reimagining of a classic lemon tart disrupted during preparation. The deconstructed dessert reflects Bottura's avant-garde approach, challenging conventions while paying homage to the essence of traditional flavors.

Beyond his culinary prowess, Bottura is recognized for his commitment to social issues. His "Food for Soul" project aims to combat food waste and promote social inclusion by transforming surplus ingredients into nourishing meals for vulnerable communities. Bottura's influence extends beyond the kitchen, inspiring a new generation of chefs to marry creativity with a sense of social responsibility.

Heston Blumenthal: The Alchemist of Molecular Gastronomy

In the realm of molecular gastronomy, Heston Blumenthal stands as a pioneer, transforming the culinary landscape with his avant-garde approach to cooking. The British chef, known for his experimental techniques and scientific exploration of food, has earned acclaim for his restaurant, The Fat Duck, which holds three Michelin stars.

Blumenthal's iconic dish, "Bacon and Egg Ice Cream," exemplifies his approach to molecular gastronomy. The dessert, which resembles a classic English breakfast, features a scoop of bacon-flavored ice cream served with a sphere of egg custard. The dish challenges preconceptions of flavor and texture, showcasing Blumenthal's ability to surprise and delight diners.

Beyond his innovative creations, Blumenthal is a proponent of understanding the science behind cooking. His curiosity-driven approach has led to collaborations with food scientists and explorations into the psychology of taste. Blumenthal's influence extends to both professional chefs and home cooks, inspiring a new appreciation for the intersection of science and culinary artistry.

Enrique Olvera: The Modern Interpreter of Mexican Cuisine

Enrique Olvera, a trailblazing chef from Mexico, has become a global ambassador for Mexican cuisine, marrying tradition with innovation. His restaurant, Pujol, located in Mexico City, has earned acclaim for its modern interpretations of traditional Mexican dishes, showcasing Olvera's commitment to preserving the essence of local flavors.

One of Olvera's iconic dishes, "Mole Madre," is a testament to his reverence for Mexican culinary heritage. The dish features a complex mole sauce that has been continuously aged for over 1,500 days, demonstrating Olvera's dedication to time-honored techniques and flavors. The dish pays homage to the rich tapestry of Mexican ingredients and culinary traditions.

Olvera's impact extends beyond the kitchen; he is a vocal advocate for sustainability and ethical sourcing of ingredients. Through initiatives like "Mesa para Todos," he works to address food insecurity and promote sustainable practices within the culinary industry. Olvera's modern interpretations of Mexican cuisine celebrate the depth and diversity of his country's culinary heritage.

Conclusion: Masterful Legacies on the Plate

In conclusion, these chef legends—Jiro Ono, Julia Child, Massimo Bottura, Heston Blumenthal, and Enrique Olvera—have left an indelible mark on the culinary world, shaping iconic dishes that transcend time and cultural boundaries. Their creativity, innovation, and dedication have not only elevated the art of cooking but have also inspired generations of chefs to push the boundaries of flavor, technique, and culinary storytelling. As we savor the iconic dishes associated with these chefs, we celebrate the enduring legacies they have crafted on the global plate.

Artful Plating: Discuss the aesthetics of iconic dishes and presentation.

In the realm of gastronomy, the presentation of a dish is an art form that extends beyond taste, engaging the senses through visual allure and artistic expression. Artful plating is the culinary language that transforms a meal into a visual masterpiece, elevating iconic dishes to an immersive experience that captivates diners from the moment the plate is set before them. In this exploration of iconic dishes, we delve into the world of artful plating, unraveling the stories and techniques behind the visual aesthetics that enhance the dining experience.

Sushi as Canvas: The Aesthetics of Japanese Precision

The art of sushi plating exemplifies the Japanese philosophy of precision, balance, and reverence for nature's beauty. Each piece of sushi is meticulously crafted, with the chef considering not only flavor but also color, texture, and form. The canvas is often minimalist—often a simple wooden plank or slate—allowing the sushi pieces to take center stage.

The use of vibrant, contrasting colors is a hallmark of sushi presentation. Slices of fresh sashimi-grade fish, delicate rolls, and artfully arranged garnishes create a visual symphony. Wasabi and pickled ginger serve not only as palate cleansers but also as elements contributing to the overall color palette.

The art of nigiri—a small hand-pressed mound of rice topped with a slice of fish—is a study in simplicity and elegance. Chefs carefully mold the rice, ensuring a delicate balance of textures, and then crown it with precisely sliced fish. The result is a visual harmony that mirrors the refined flavors of each bite.

Beyond the plate, the use of traditional serveware, such as lacquered trays and bamboo mats, adds an extra layer of aesthetic appeal. The arrangement of sushi on these vessels reflects the interconnectedness of culinary art and Japanese cultural aesthetics, creating a dining experience that is not just a meal but a visual journey.

Pizza Napoletana: A Visual Symphony of Freshness

The iconic Neapolitan pizza, with its simple yet flavorful components, is a testament to the visual appeal of rustic authenticity. In the realm of pizza plating, less is often more, allowing the vibrant colors and textures of the ingredients to shine. The canvas is a round, slightly charred crust, and the toppings become the palette for a visual symphony.

Tomato sauce, made from ripe San Marzano tomatoes, is applied with a deft hand, creating a base that is both flavorful and visually striking. Fresh mozzarella, torn into irregular pieces, adds a dynamic element that contrasts with the uniformity of the tomato sauce. The final touch—a scattering of basil leaves—brings a burst of green, completing the tricolor composition reminiscent of the Italian flag.

The use of a wood-fired oven imparts a visual and textural element to the crust, with blistering and charring contributing to the rustic charm. The finished pizza, served on a round wooden board, becomes a work of edible art that invites diners to savor not only the flavors but also the visual narrative of its creation.

The visual appeal of Neapolitan pizza extends beyond its iconic Margherita rendition. Variations like the Marinara, adorned with garlic, oregano, and a drizzle of olive oil, showcase the beauty of simplicity. The careful placement of each ingredient creates a balanced composition, inviting diners to appreciate the visual harmony before indulging in the culinary experience.

Biryani Elegance: Layers of Flavor, Layers of Presentation

Biryani, a dish celebrated for its aromatic layers and rich flavors, takes on an exquisite visual identity through the art of plating. The traditional presentation of biryani involves serving it in a large, communal dish, often a handi or a copper vessel. The unveiling of the biryani becomes a theatrical moment, enticing diners with the promise of layers waiting to be discovered.

The top layer of biryani is adorned with fragrant saffron-infused rice, creating a canvas of golden hues. The choice of protein—be it succulent pieces of meat, tender chicken, or flavorful vegetables—adds a contrasting element to the palette. The scattered fried onions on top provide a crispy texture and contribute to the visual depth of the dish.

As the lid is lifted, the aromatic steam rises, carrying the essence of spices and herbs. The layers of rice and protein are revealed, each bite promising a symphony of flavors meticulously layered during the cooking process. The garnish of fresh coriander leaves and mint adds a burst of green, enhancing the visual appeal and providing a refreshing contrast to the richness of the dish.

In the realm of biryani, regional variations introduce diverse visual elements. The Kolkata Biryani, with its inclusion of boiled eggs and fragrant potatoes, adds an extra layer of complexity to the presentation. The Hyderabadi Dum Biryani, cooked in a sealed pot, emphasizes the art of layering, with the flavors of rice, meat, and spices melding into a visual and culinary masterpiece.

Croissant Elegance: Layers Unveiled

The iconic croissant, with its delicate layers and buttery aroma, presents a unique canvas for artful plating in the realm of pastries. The visual allure of a well-crafted croissant lies in the precise laminated layers, achieved through the meticulous folding of dough and butter. The exterior, golden and flaky, promises a sensory experience that transcends taste.

Traditional croissants are often presented on a simple, elegant plate or a pastry display, allowing the layers to take center stage. The crescent shape, with its defined curves and golden sheen, adds a touch of elegance. The dusting of powdered sugar or a light glaze enhances the visual appeal, creating a glistening finish that invites the eye to explore the layers within.

Variations of croissants, such as almond croissants or pain au chocolat, introduce additional visual elements. The almond croissant, adorned with slivered almonds and a dusting of confectioners' sugar, showcases the play between textures and flavors. Pain au chocolat, with its hidden core of rich chocolate, invites diners to savor the visual surprise as they bite into the flaky layers.

The visual appeal of croissants extends beyond the pastry itself to the ritual of serving. Pastry chefs often take care in arranging a selection of croissants on a tiered stand or a wooden board, creating an inviting tableau. The artful presentation of croissants in a bakery or cafe setting is an integral part of the experience, inviting customers to appreciate not only the taste but also the craftsmanship behind each flaky layer.

Tacos: Colorful and Contrasting Compositions

In the world of tacos, artful plating is a celebration of colors, textures, and contrasts. Whether served street-style on a simple paper plate or presented in a high-end restaurant, the visual appeal of tacos lies in their vibrant and dynamic compositions. The taco becomes a canvas for a culinary palette that reflects the diversity of Mexican flavors.

The choice of tortilla, whether corn or flour, sets the tone for the visual composition. The warm tones of a freshly pressed corn tortilla provide a backdrop for the colorful array of fillings. Flour tortillas, with their pale hue, create a neutral canvas that allows the ingredients to pop visually. The tacos are often served in multiples, creating a visually appealing arrangement that invites diners to mix and match flavors.

The artful placement of fillings is a key element in taco presentation. Grilled meats, adorned with charred edges, are often layered with fresh, crisp vegetables and vibrant salsas. The finishing touch of cilantro leaves, a squeeze of lime, and a sprinkle of diced onions adds a burst of freshness and visual appeal. The use of colorful garnishes, such as radishes or pickled onions, further enhances the overall composition.

In upscale taco restaurants, chefs elevate the art of plating by focusing on precision and visual balance. Each taco becomes a miniature masterpiece, with carefully arranged components that showcase the culinary artistry behind the dish. The use of elevated serveware, such as sleek plates or custom-designed vessels, adds an extra layer of sophistication to the taco presentation.

Conclusion: The Visual Feast of Iconic Dishes

In conclusion, the art of plating transforms iconic dishes into visual feasts that engage diners on a multisensory level. Whether it's the precision of sushi presentation, the rustic charm of Neapolitan pizza, the layered elegance of biryani, the delicate beauty of croissants, or the vibrant compositions of tacos, each iconic dish tells a visual story that enhances the overall dining experience. The artful plating of these dishes not only delights the eyes but also serves as a testament to the craftsmanship, creativity, and cultural significance embedded in the culinary world. As we savor these iconic creations, we partake in a visual journey that complements the rich narratives and flavors encapsulated within each dish.

Modern Twists: Highlight contemporary reinterpretations of traditional iconic dishes.

In the dynamic world of gastronomy, the evolution of iconic dishes is not confined to tradition but extends into the realm of innovation and reinterpretation. Modern twists on classic favorites breathe new life into culinary traditions, infusing them with creativity, unexpected flavors, and cutting-edge techniques. As we explore the landscape of iconic dishes, we delve into the realm of modern twists—contemporary reinterpretations that pay homage to the past while embracing the spirit of culinary exploration.

Sushi Unbound: Beyond Tradition

In the traditional realm of sushi, where precision and adherence to centuries-old techniques are revered, modern chefs are pushing boundaries, introducing unexpected ingredients, and challenging the conventional notions of what sushi can be. The result is a wave of contemporary reinterpretations that honor the essence of sushi while inviting diners on a journey of culinary innovation.

One such modern twist is the introduction of non-traditional proteins, from wagyu beef to foie gras, taking center stage in sushi creations. The interplay of textures and flavors between the marbled richness of wagyu and the delicate balance of rice and seaweed showcases the adaptability of sushi to diverse culinary influences.

The fusion of global flavors is another avenue explored in modern sushi reinterpretations. From Mexican-inspired rolls featuring spicy salsas and avocado to Mediterranean-infused sushi with olive tapenade and sun-dried tomatoes, chefs are weaving a tapestry of diverse influences into the traditional sushi canvas. These bold combinations redefine the boundaries of sushi, turning it into a cross-cultural culinary experience.

Technological advancements also play a role in modern sushi twists. Chefs experiment with molecular gastronomy techniques, incorporating elements like sous-vide-cooked rice, foams, and edible films. These innovations not only showcase a commitment to pushing culinary boundaries but also create an immersive dining experience that engages multiple senses.

The modern sushi landscape challenges purists and enthusiasts alike to embrace a broader definition of this iconic dish, one that celebrates tradition while embracing the ever-evolving nature of global gastronomy.

Pizza Reinvented: Beyond the Margherita

While the classic Margherita pizza remains a timeless favorite, contemporary chefs are reimagining pizza in ways that defy tradition and elevate this iconic dish to new heights. Modern twists on pizza incorporate unconventional toppings, alternative bases, and inventive flavor profiles that challenge the familiar yet comforting appeal of the traditional pie.

One trend in modern pizza reinterpretations is the exploration of diverse toppings that go beyond the standard pepperoni or mushrooms. Chefs experiment with unexpected ingredients like truffle oil, smoked salmon, or even tropical fruits, creating a sensory adventure that surprises and delights the palate. The artisanal approach to sourcing and preparing toppings elevates the overall quality and flavor complexity.

Creative reinterpretations also extend to the pizza crust itself. Cauliflower crusts, gluten-free options, and charcoal-infused dough are just a few examples of contemporary twists on the traditional pizza base. These variations cater to evolving dietary preferences while introducing new textures and flavors to the pizza experience.

In the realm of flavor profiles, chefs are exploring global influences, infusing pizzas with ingredients and spices from diverse culinary traditions. Indian-inspired curries, Thai-influenced coconut milk bases, or Middle Eastern spice blends add a multicultural dimension to pizza, reflecting the interconnected nature of the global culinary landscape.

Modern pizzerias often emphasize the importance of craftsmanship, using high-quality, locally sourced ingredients and innovative techniques. Wood-fired ovens, house-made sauces, and artisanal cheese blends contribute to a refined pizza experience that transcends the casual connotations often associated with this iconic dish.

The reinvention of pizza showcases a dynamic interplay between tradition and innovation, inviting diners to embark on a culinary journey that celebrates the enduring popularity of this beloved comfort food while embracing the creative possibilities that modern gastronomy offers.

Biryani Redefined: Contemporary Layers of Flavor

In the world of biryani, a dish steeped in tradition and culinary heritage, contemporary chefs are redefining the boundaries, introducing novel ingredients, and playing with techniques to create modern twists that honor the essence of the dish while offering a fresh perspective.

One avenue of reinterpretation is the introduction of alternative proteins. While traditional biryani is often associated with chicken, mutton, or beef, modern twists incorporate seafood, plant-based proteins, or exotic meats. The substitution of traditional proteins with ingredients like prawns, jackfruit, or even quail brings new textures and flavors to the biryani experience.

Chefs are also experimenting with the rice component, exploring heirloom varieties, or incorporating ancient grains to add nutritional depth and nuanced flavors. The choice of rice, its parboiling techniques, and the integration of aromatic herbs elevate the biryani to a sophisticated culinary creation.

Modern biryani reinterpretations embrace global influences, infusing the dish with ingredients and spices from diverse culinary traditions. Thai basil, Spanish saffron, or Mexican chili peppers contribute to a fusion of flavors that transcends regional boundaries, reflecting the interconnected nature of contemporary gastronomy.

Innovative cooking methods, such as sous-vide preparation or slow-cooking in vacuum-sealed bags, introduce precise control over the textures and flavors of the ingredients. These modern techniques enhance the overall dining experience, offering a sensory journey that goes beyond the familiar aromas of traditional biryani.

While respecting the cultural significance of biryani, contemporary reinterpretations celebrate the spirit of experimentation, inviting diners to savor the layers of tradition and innovation in every aromatic bite.

Croissant Fusion: Global Flavors, Local Pastry

The classic croissant, with its buttery layers and flaky texture, has become a canvas for culinary experimentation as chefs introduce global flavors and unique twists to this iconic pastry. Modern interpretations of croissants go beyond the traditional boundaries, incorporating diverse ingredients and innovative techniques.

One prominent trend in croissant reinvention is the fusion of global flavors. Chefs draw inspiration from international cuisines to create unique fillings and toppings that challenge the expectations associated with this French pastry. Matcha-infused croissants, filled with layers of green tea-flavored cream, or chai-spiced varieties, featuring aromatic Indian spices, showcase a fusion of culinary traditions that resonates with contemporary palates.

Contemporary croissants also explore alternative doughs, incorporating whole grains, ancient flours, or even colored doughs to add visual interest and depth of flavor. These variations not only cater to diverse dietary preferences but also contribute to the overall sensory experience of enjoying a modern croissant.

Inventive fillings play a pivotal role in modern croissant reinterpretations. From indulgent options like salted caramel or dark chocolate ganache to savory combinations like prosciutto and cheese or truffle-infused cream, the modern croissant becomes a versatile canvas for sweet and savory expressions alike.

Artistic presentations elevate the modern croissant experience, with chefs using creative techniques for shaping, folding, and layering. The traditional crescent shape is sometimes abandoned in favor of innovative forms, such as braided twists or stuffed pockets, showcasing the skill and artistry of pastry chefs.

As the croissant continues to be a symbol of indulgence and sophistication, its modern reinterpretations pay homage to tradition while embracing the global diversity of culinary influences, creating a delightful fusion of old-world charm and contemporary creativity.

Taco Fusion: Crossing Culinary Borders

Tacos, a cornerstone of Mexican street food, have become a playground for culinary experimentation as chefs introduce contemporary twists that transcend traditional boundaries. Modern interpretations of tacos reimagine the classic format, infusing global flavors, alternative proteins, and inventive techniques that celebrate the versatility of this iconic dish.

One avenue of modern taco reinterpretation is the incorporation of global flavors and ingredients. Tacos now feature eclectic combinations such as Korean barbecue tacos with bulgogi-style beef, kimchi, and gochujang aioli or Mediterranean-inspired options with grilled lamb, tzatziki, and pickled vegetables. These fusion creations reflect the interconnected nature of the global culinary landscape, offering a diverse and dynamic taco experience.

Alternative proteins play a significant role in modern taco twists, with chefs exploring plant-based options, exotic meats, or seafood to add variety and innovation to the traditional taco lineup. Jackfruit carnitas, seared ahi tuna, or smoked tofu fillings demonstrate a commitment to culinary creativity and a willingness to push the boundaries of taco tradition.

Innovative cooking techniques also contribute to the modern taco experience. Chefs experiment with sous-vide preparation, slow-cooking, or unconventional grilling methods to enhance the flavors and textures of taco components. These techniques not only showcase culinary skill but also elevate the overall dining experience for taco enthusiasts.

Artful presentation is a key element in modern taco reinterpretations, with chefs using creative plating techniques and unique serveware to showcase the diversity of flavors and ingredients. Tacos are often arranged in visually appealing compositions, inviting diners to savor not only the taste but also the artistry behind each bite.

As modern tacos continue to evolve, they remain a symbol of culinary innovation and cultural exchange, bridging the gap between tradition and contemporary creativity. These reinterpretations celebrate the timeless appeal of tacos while inviting diners on a global journey through the diverse and flavorful world of modern taco creations.

Conclusion: The Ever-Evolving Palate

In conclusion, the modern twists on iconic dishes represent a dynamic interplay between culinary tradition and innovation. Sushi, pizza, biryani, croissants, and tacos undergo creative reinterpretations that celebrate the enduring popularity of these dishes while embracing the ever-evolving palate of contemporary gastronomy. As chefs push boundaries, experiment with global flavors, and introduce cutting-edge techniques, the culinary landscape expands, inviting diners to embark on a journey of discovery, where the familiar becomes extraordinary, and the iconic becomes a canvas for the infinite possibilities of taste and creativity.

Chapter 4: Innovations and Trends
Cutting-Edge Techniques: Explore modern culinary innovations, including molecular gastronomy.

In the ever-evolving realm of gastronomy, chefs are at the forefront of innovation, constantly pushing the boundaries of traditional cooking techniques. One of the most transformative movements in recent culinary history is the advent of molecular gastronomy—an avant-garde approach that blends science and art to create unprecedented dining experiences. As we delve into the world of cutting-edge techniques, this exploration focuses on molecular gastronomy, unraveling its principles, impact on culinary creativity, and the sensory wonders it brings to the table.

Understanding Molecular Gastronomy: A Scientific Culinary Symphony

Molecular gastronomy is a discipline that marries scientific principles with culinary artistry, aiming to understand the physical and chemical transformations that occur during cooking. Pioneered by scientists such as Hervé This and chefs like Ferran Adrià and Heston Blumenthal, this innovative approach seeks to deconstruct and reconstruct traditional dishes, challenging preconceived notions of taste, texture, and presentation.

At its core, molecular gastronomy explores the interplay of food components at a molecular level. Techniques such as spherification, gelification, foaming, and emulsification are employed to manipulate the physical and chemical properties of ingredients. The result is a culinary symphony that goes beyond conventional cooking methods, inviting diners to experience food in ways previously unimaginable.

Spherification: Culinary Caviar and Beyond

One of the hallmark techniques of molecular gastronomy is spherification—a process that transforms liquid ingredients into gelatinous spheres resembling caviar. Developed by Ferran Adrià, this technique has become a symbol of avant-garde culinary innovation, offering chefs a novel way to present and consume liquids.

The process involves the use of sodium alginate and calcium chloride. The liquid to be spherified is mixed with sodium alginate, creating a base solution. This solution is then carefully dropped into a bath of calcium chloride, causing the liquid to form a thin membrane, encapsulating the contents. The result is delicate spheres bursting with flavor, adding a visually striking and texturally intriguing element to dishes.

Spherification opens the door to endless creative possibilities. From encapsulating fruit juices to infusing broths with unexpected flavors, chefs use this technique to surprise and delight diners. The culinary world has witnessed the emergence of "caviar" made from balsamic vinegar, olive oil, or even cocktails, offering a playful and inventive twist on familiar flavors.

Gelification: Transforming Textures with Precision

Gelification is another key technique within the realm of molecular gastronomy, allowing chefs to control and manipulate the texture of ingredients. Whether creating fluid gels, gel noodles, or gel sheets, this technique provides a canvas for culinary experimentation, transforming traditional textures into avant-garde delights.

Agar-agar and gellan gum are commonly used gelling agents in molecular gastronomy. These substances react to temperature changes, enabling chefs to create gels with various consistencies. By carefully adjusting the concentration of gelling agents and the temperature of the liquid, chefs can achieve textures ranging from a delicate gel to a firm, rubbery consistency.

The applications of gelification are diverse. In savory dishes, chefs may create gel sheets to encase delicate seafood or form gel noodles to add a playful element to a soup. In desserts, gelification allows for the creation of intricate gelatinous layers, transforming classic treats into visually stunning and texturally rich experiences.

Foaming: Airy Delights and Culinary Clouds

Foaming is a technique that introduces air into liquid ingredients, creating stable foam with a light and airy texture. This method, often associated with whipping siphons or nitrous oxide chargers, has become a signature element in molecular gastronomy, elevating both savory and sweet dishes to new heights.

The key to successful foaming lies in achieving the right balance of ingredients and aeration. Chefs may use ingredients like lecithin, a natural cmulsifier, to stabilize the foam and prevent it from collapsing. The result is a cloud-like structure that adds a whimsical and ethereal quality to the dish.

In savory applications, foaming may involve creating foamy sauces or emulsions to enhance the mouthfeel and visual appeal of a dish. In desserts, chefs may craft foamy toppings for beverages, create light and airy mousses, or even fashion foamy ice cream accompaniments. The versatility of foaming allows chefs to experiment with texture and presentation, offering diners a multi-sensory experience.

Emulsification: Transforming Textures and Enhancing Flavors

Emulsification, a traditional culinary technique, takes on new dimensions in the realm of molecular gastronomy. This process involves combining liquids that typically do not mix, such as oil and water, to create stable and smooth emulsions. Chefs utilize modern emulsification techniques to enhance flavors, transform textures, and introduce unexpected elements to their creations.

Molecular gastronomy introduces unique emulsifiers, such as soy lecithin, that enable chefs to create stable emulsions with minimal effort. This opens the door to creating foams, airs, and other innovative textures in both savory and sweet applications.

In savory dishes, emulsification may involve the creation of flavorful emulsified sauces or vinaigrettes with a velvety texture. The stable nature of these emulsions allows for precise control over the mouthfeel and presentation of the dish. In desserts, emulsification can be used to craft creamy and smooth textures in ice creams, mousses, or sauces, adding a layer of sophistication to traditional favorites.

Impact of Molecular Gastronomy on Culinary Creativity

Molecular gastronomy has profoundly impacted the way chefs approach culinary creativity. By providing a scientific understanding of cooking processes, this discipline empowers chefs to experiment with textures, presentations, and flavor combinations that were once unimaginable. The result is a culinary landscape that embraces innovation, pushing the boundaries of traditional techniques and challenging the expectations of diners.

The use of molecular gastronomy in high-end gastronomic establishments has become a symbol of culinary avant-garde, attracting both curiosity and acclaim. Chefs who embrace these cutting-edge techniques often engage in a delicate dance between art and science, seeking to surprise and captivate diners while maintaining a deep respect for the fundamentals of taste and balance.

One of the notable impacts of molecular gastronomy is the elevation of the dining experience to a multisensory adventure. Diners are not only treated to exquisite flavors but also to visually stunning presentations and unexpected textures. Molecular gastronomy transforms the act of eating into a form of entertainment, inviting diners to engage with their food on a level that transcends the traditional boundaries of the culinary experience.

Challenges and Criticisms of Molecular Gastronomy

While molecular gastronomy has gained widespread acclaim, it is not without its challenges and criticisms. Some critics argue that the emphasis on scientific precision may overshadow the intuitive and improvisational aspects of cooking that define traditional culinary practices. Others express concerns about the reliance on specialized equipment and ingredients, making these techniques inaccessible to many chefs and home cooks.

The use of certain chemicals and additives in molecular gastronomy has also sparked debates about food safety and health implications. Some critics question the long-term effects of consuming dishes created with these innovative techniques, prompting discussions about the responsibility of chefs to prioritize both innovation and well-being.

Despite these challenges and criticisms, molecular gastronomy continues to evolve and inspire chefs worldwide. Many practitioners emphasize the importance of balance, integrating modern techniques with traditional wisdom to create a harmonious dining experience. As the culinary world embraces diversity and experimentation, molecular gastronomy remains a fascinating chapter in the ongoing narrative of gastronomic evolution.

Conclusion: A Culinary Frontier Unveiled

In conclusion, the exploration of cutting-edge techniques, with a focus on molecular gastronomy, unveils a culinary frontier where science and art converge. Spherification, gelification, foaming, and emulsification represent just a few facets of the innovative techniques that chefs employ to push the boundaries of traditional cooking. Molecular gastronomy has not only transformed the way we perceive and consume food but has also opened a realm of endless possibilities for culinary creativity. As chefs continue to experiment, adapt, and embrace the scientific principles that underpin these techniques, the world of gastronomy remains in a state of perpetual evolution, inviting diners to embark on a thrilling journey through the ever-expanding universe of taste, texture, and culinary wonder.

Sustainable Practices: Discuss eco-friendly practices shaping the culinary world.

As the world grapples with environmental challenges, the culinary industry is undergoing a transformative shift towards sustainability. Chefs, restaurants, and food enthusiasts are increasingly recognizing the need for eco-friendly practices that not only preserve the planet but also enhance the quality and ethics of the culinary experience. This exploration delves into the realm of sustainable practices, examining how conscientious choices in sourcing, production, and consumption are shaping the future of gastronomy.

Embracing the Farm-to-Table Movement

The farm-to-table movement stands as a beacon of sustainability within the culinary landscape, championing a direct and transparent supply chain from local farmers to consumers. This practice not only reduces the carbon footprint associated with food transportation but also supports local economies and promotes the use of seasonal, fresh ingredients.

Farm-to-table chefs prioritize partnerships with local farmers, cultivating relationships that extend beyond transactional exchanges. By sourcing directly from nearby farms, restaurants can offer dishes that showcase the authentic flavors of the region while fostering a sense of community and trust. This commitment to local sourcing not only elevates the quality of ingredients but also contributes to a more sustainable and resilient food system.

Reducing Food Waste: From Root to Stem

Addressing the issue of food waste has become a critical aspect of sustainable culinary practices. Chefs are embracing the "root to stem" philosophy, utilizing the entirety of ingredients to minimize waste and maximize flavor. This approach encourages creativity in the kitchen, prompting chefs to explore innovative uses for parts of fruits, vegetables, and herbs that may traditionally be discarded.

Root-to-stem cooking involves techniques such as pickling watermelon rinds, turning carrot tops into pesto, or transforming citrus peels into zesty infusions. By adopting a holistic approach to ingredient utilization, chefs not only contribute to environmental conservation but also demonstrate the culinary potential inherent in every part of a plant.

Restaurants are also implementing strategies to reduce plate waste, such as offering flexible portion sizes, encouraging sharing, or providing options for patrons to take home leftovers. These initiatives not only align with sustainability goals but also resonate with diners who value conscientious dining experiences.

The Rise of Plant-Based Cuisine

The surge in popularity of plant-based cuisine represents a seismic shift towards sustainability within the culinary world. Beyond catering to dietary preferences, the embrace of plant-based dishes reflects a commitment to reducing the environmental impact of food production, particularly in the context of meat and dairy consumption.

Chefs are exploring the versatility of plant-based ingredients, crafting innovative and flavorful dishes that challenge preconceived notions about vegetarian and vegan cuisine. Plant-based proteins, such as tofu, tempeh, and seitan, are being transformed into delectable creations that rival their meat counterparts in taste and texture.

The adoption of plant-based menus not only aligns with sustainability goals but also responds to the growing awareness of the environmental consequences associated with industrial meat production. By diversifying menus with plant-centric options, restaurants contribute to the reduction of greenhouse gas emissions, land degradation, and water consumption linked to traditional livestock farming.

Eco-Friendly Cooking Techniques

In addition to conscious sourcing and plant-based menus, chefs are reevaluating cooking techniques to align with sustainable practices. Energy-efficient appliances, induction cooktops, and convection ovens are becoming staples in eco-friendly kitchens, reducing energy consumption and minimizing environmental impact.

Chefs are also exploring alternative cooking methods that prioritize sustainability without compromising flavor. Techniques such as sous-vide cooking, which reduces food waste and energy use, or solar cooking, harnessing the power of the sun for slow and steady preparation, exemplify the innovative approaches chefs are adopting to minimize their ecological footprint.

Furthermore, the use of sustainable cookware and utensils, such as those made from recycled or biodegradable materials, adds another layer to the eco-conscious kitchen. These choices reflect a holistic commitment to sustainability, extending beyond ingredient selection to every aspect of the culinary process.

Local and Sustainable Seafood Practices

The conscientious sourcing of seafood is a crucial component of sustainable culinary practices. Overfishing, destructive fishing methods, and habitat degradation pose significant threats to marine ecosystems. Chefs and consumers alike are increasingly turning to sustainable seafood options to support responsible fishing practices and preserve marine biodiversity.

Seafood sustainability involves choosing fish and shellfish species that are abundant, well-managed, and harvested using methods that minimize environmental impact. Certification programs, such as the Marine Stewardship Council (MSC) and the Aquaculture Stewardship Council (ASC), play a vital role in guiding consumers and chefs towards sustainable seafood choices.

Chefs are collaborating with local fishermen and fisheries that prioritize sustainable practices, establishing relationships built on environmental stewardship and mutual respect. By featuring responsibly sourced seafood on their menus, chefs contribute to the preservation of ocean ecosystems while offering diners a conscientious and flavorful dining experience.

Waste Reduction in the Culinary Industry

Efforts to reduce waste extend beyond the kitchen and into the broader operations of the culinary industry. Restaurants are adopting strategies to minimize single-use plastics, implement recycling programs, and repurpose waste materials. Initiatives such as composting organic waste or donating surplus food to local charities exemplify the commitment to holistic waste reduction.

Chefs are embracing creativity in reimagining waste materials. Coffee grounds find new life as ingredients in desserts, spent grains from brewing contribute to artisanal bread recipes, and fruit peels become flavorful infusions. These innovative approaches not only minimize waste but also showcase the resourcefulness and ingenuity of chefs committed to sustainable culinary practices.

The Impact of Sustainable Certifications

The emergence of sustainable certifications and labels has played a significant role in guiding both chefs and consumers towards environmentally friendly choices. Certifications such as USDA Organic, Fair Trade, and Rainforest Alliance provide assurance that ingredients meet specific environmental and ethical standards.

Restaurants showcasing these certifications on their menus signal their commitment to sustainability, offering transparency and accountability to diners who prioritize eco-friendly choices. The visibility of such certifications not only informs consumers but also fosters a sense of trust between chefs and their patrons.

Challenges and Opportunities in Sustainable Culinary Practices

While the adoption of sustainable practices in the culinary world is gaining momentum, it comes with its own set of challenges and opportunities. Sourcing local and sustainable ingredients may pose logistical challenges for chefs, requiring them to build robust networks with local farmers and producers. Additionally, the cost implications of sustainable practices can present financial hurdles for some establishments, necessitating a delicate balance between ethical choices and economic viability.

However, the challenges are met with a host of opportunities. The rise in consumer awareness and demand for sustainable dining experiences creates a market for restaurants that prioritize eco-friendly practices. Chefs are discovering that sustainable choices often lead to heightened creativity, as the constraints of working with seasonal, local ingredients inspire innovative approaches to menu development.

Conclusion: A Greener Culinary Future

In conclusion, the integration of sustainable practices into the culinary world marks a pivotal moment in gastronomic evolution. From conscientious sourcing and waste reduction to embracing plant-based cuisine and eco-friendly cooking techniques, chefs are leading the way towards a greener and more ethical culinary future. The choices made in kitchens today not only shape the flavors on our plates but also contribute to the preservation of the planet for future generations. As the culinary industry continues to navigate the intersection of taste, ethics, and environmental responsibility, the journey towards sustainability unfolds as a delicious and fulfilling exploration of culinary possibilities.

Tech in Cooking: Examine the influence of technology on cooking methods.

In the contemporary culinary landscape, technology has become an integral partner in the kitchen, revolutionizing traditional cooking methods and shaping the way chefs approach their craft. This exploration dives into the multifaceted relationship between technology and cooking, uncovering the innovative tools, techniques, and trends that are reshaping the gastronomic experience.

Precision and Consistency: Sous Vide Revolution

Sous vide, a cooking technique that originated in the 1970s, has experienced a renaissance in recent years, thanks to advancements in technology. This method involves vacuum-sealing food in plastic pouches and cooking it in a water bath at precisely controlled temperatures for an extended period. The result is food that is evenly cooked to the desired level of doneness, with unmatched precision and consistency.

Sous vide technology has evolved with the introduction of immersion circulators and precision water baths. These devices allow chefs to maintain precise control over the cooking temperature, ensuring that proteins, vegetables, and even desserts are cooked to perfection. The sous vide method has found applications in both professional kitchens and home cooking, providing a foolproof way to achieve restaurant-quality results.

Beyond precision, sous vide cooking has become a tool for innovation. Chefs experiment with flavor infusions, marinating ingredients within the vacuum-sealed pouches to intensify taste. The method also allows for unique texture modifications, such as achieving buttery tenderness in meats while preserving their natural juices.

Revolutionizing Texture: Molecular Gastronomy and Texture Transformations

Molecular gastronomy, a discipline that fuses science and culinary arts, has introduced groundbreaking techniques that redefine the textures of food. From foams and gels to powders and spheres, chefs utilize technology to create imaginative textures that challenge conventional culinary norms.

The spherification process, which transforms liquids into gelatinous spheres, exemplifies the texture-centric approach of molecular gastronomy. By manipulating the molecular properties of ingredients, chefs can craft caviar-like pearls bursting with flavor or encapsulate liquids within delicate membranes, introducing a playful and unexpected dimension to dishes.

Gelification, another key technique within molecular gastronomy, allows chefs to control the texture of ingredients, creating gels with a range of consistencies. This technology-driven method enables chefs to present foods in novel forms, from fluid gels and gel noodles to intricate gel sheets that elevate both visual and textural aspects of a dish.

In the pursuit of texture mastery, chefs explore various hydrocolloids, emulsifiers, and gelling agents, experimenting with combinations that produce unique sensations in the mouth. Molecular gastronomy's influence on texture extends beyond avant-garde dining establishments, inspiring a broader culinary conversation about the interplay between taste, aroma, and mouthfeel.

Connected Kitchens: Smart Appliances and IoT Integration

The advent of smart kitchen appliances and the integration of the Internet of Things (IoT) have ushered in a new era of connectivity in the culinary world. Smart ovens, refrigerators, and cooking devices can be controlled remotely via mobile apps, allowing chefs to monitor and adjust cooking processes from anywhere.

Smart ovens, equipped with sensors and cameras, offer features like recipe recognition and automated cooking adjustments. This technology not only enhances convenience but also ensures optimal cooking results by adapting to the specific characteristics of ingredients. Additionally, smart ovens can provide real-time updates to users, allowing them to track the cooking progress without being physically present in the kitchen.

Refrigerators with IoT integration go beyond traditional temperature control, offering features such as inventory tracking, expiration alerts, and recipe suggestions based on available ingredients. These smart appliances contribute to reducing food waste by promoting better organization and awareness of the ingredients stored.

Connected kitchens also extend to smart cooking devices, such as precision cookers and multicookers. These devices leverage technology to simplify complex cooking techniques, providing users with precise temperature control, step-by-step guided recipes, and automated cooking programs. The accessibility of smart cooking devices has democratized advanced culinary techniques, empowering home cooks to explore new flavors and textures with confidence.

Culinary Creativity Unleashed: 3D Food Printing

The intersection of technology and culinary arts has given rise to 3D food printing, a cutting-edge innovation that holds the potential to transform the way we conceptualize and produce food. 3D food printers use edible materials, often in the form of pastes or gels, to create intricate and customized food designs layer by layer.

One of the key advantages of 3D food printing is its ability to produce visually stunning and precisely engineered dishes. Chefs can design intricate structures, intricate patterns, and personalized shapes that would be challenging to achieve through traditional means. This technology opens new possibilities for artistic expression and presentation in the culinary world.

Beyond aesthetics, 3D food printing introduces opportunities for flavor modulation. By layering different ingredients or textures, chefs can create complex and dynamic taste experiences within a single dish. Customization reaches new heights as chefs tailor the composition and arrangement of ingredients to suit individual preferences.

While 3D food printing is still in its early stages of adoption, it represents a promising frontier for culinary creativity. As the technology continues to evolve, it holds the potential to redefine the relationship between chefs, diners, and the culinary canvas.

Innovative Cooking Surfaces: Induction and Beyond

Advancements in cooking surfaces have significantly impacted the efficiency and precision of modern kitchens. Induction cooktops, in particular, have gained popularity for their rapid heating, precise temperature control, and energy efficiency. These cooktops utilize magnetic fields to directly heat the cookware, offering a safer and more responsive cooking experience.

Induction technology not only enhances safety but also provides chefs with greater control over the cooking process. Instant adjustments to temperature settings, rapid boiling, and precise simmering contribute to the overall efficiency of the kitchen. Additionally, the absence of an open flame or exposed heating elements reduces the risk of accidents and makes induction cooktops suitable for diverse kitchen settings.

Innovative cooking surfaces extend beyond induction, with technologies like infrared cooking and plancha griddles gaining traction. Infrared cooking uses radiant heat to cook food directly, offering quick and efficient results. Plancha griddles, inspired by traditional Spanish cooking, provide a flat and versatile surface for searing, grilling, and cooking a variety of ingredients.

These technological advancements in cooking surfaces not only improve functionality but also influence the creative process in the kitchen. Chefs can experiment with different cooking techniques, temperatures, and durations, knowing that the tools at their disposal offer precise and reliable performance.

Virtual Reality and Augmented Reality: Enhancing Culinary Education

The integration of virtual reality (VR) and augmented reality (AR) into culinary education is transforming the way aspiring chefs learn and practice their craft. VR and AR applications provide immersive experiences that simulate kitchen environments, allowing users to hone their skills, experiment with recipes, and explore culinary techniques in a virtual setting.

Virtual reality applications transport users to realistic kitchen scenarios, where they can practice knife skills, execute cooking techniques, and even interact with lifelike ingredients. This hands-on approach to learning enables culinary students to develop muscle memory and confidence before entering a physical kitchen.

Augmented reality, on the other hand, overlays digital information onto the real-world kitchen environment. This technology provides real-time guidance, recipe instructions, and nutritional information as users navigate the cooking process. Chefs can visualize step-by-step procedures, ingredient measurements, and even receive instant feedback on their techniques.

The integration of VR and AR in culinary education not only enhances technical skills but also fosters creativity and adaptability. Students can explore diverse culinary traditions, virtually visit renowned kitchens, and participate in interactive culinary challenges, expanding their knowledge and perspectives.

Robotics in the Kitchen: Automating Culinary Tasks

The introduction of robotics into the kitchen has streamlined various culinary tasks, ranging from precision cutting and chopping to automated cooking processes. Robotic kitchen assistants are designed to work alongside chefs, automating repetitive tasks and enhancing overall kitchen efficiency.

Robotic chefs, equipped with advanced algorithms and sensors, can replicate precise movements and measurements, ensuring consistency in preparation. These robots are capable of performing tasks such as precision cutting, stirring, and even plating, allowing chefs to focus on creative aspects of cooking while relying on automation for repetitive actions.

The integration of robotics in commercial kitchens has the potential to revolutionize the culinary industry, particularly in high-volume settings. Automated processes can reduce labor costs, enhance food safety through precise measurements, and improve overall kitchen productivity.

While robotics in the kitchen is currently more prevalent in industrial and commercial settings, there is ongoing exploration of how these technologies can be adapted for home use. Robotic kitchen appliances and devices are emerging to assist home cooks with tasks like chopping, stirring, and even automated cooking.

Challenges and Considerations in Embracing Culinary Technology

While the integration of technology into the culinary world offers numerous benefits, it is not without its challenges and considerations. The initial cost of adopting advanced kitchen technologies, such as smart appliances or 3D food printers, may pose financial hurdles for some establishments, particularly small businesses or aspiring chefs.

Furthermore, the rapid pace of technological innovation requires chefs and culinary professionals to stay abreast of the latest developments. Continuous education and training become essential to harness the full potential of emerging technologies and incorporate them seamlessly into culinary practices.

The ethical implications of culinary technology also warrant consideration. As the industry embraces automation and robotics, questions about job displacement and the impact on traditional culinary skills come to the forefront. Balancing the advantages of efficiency and precision with the preservation of artisanal craftsmanship becomes a nuanced challenge.

Conclusion: A Technological Tapestry in the Culinary World

In conclusion, the influence of technology on cooking methods has woven a rich tapestry in the culinary world, reshaping traditions, enhancing efficiency, and unlocking new realms of creativity. From precision cooking with sous vide to the artistic possibilities of 3D food printing, chefs today navigate a landscape where technology is both a tool and a muse. As the culinary industry continues to evolve, the seamless integration of technology promises to elevate the gastronomic experience, offering chefs and food enthusiasts alike a journey of endless possibilities in taste, texture, and culinary innovation.

Street Food Trends: Explore the resurgence and global impact of street food.

In the bustling corners of cities and the vibrant markets of towns, street food has transcended its humble origins to become a global phenomenon, capturing the hearts and taste buds of millions. This exploration delves into the resurgence of street food, examining its rich history, the diverse array of flavors it offers, and the profound impact it has had on culinary landscapes around the world.

A Culinary Tapestry: The Historical Roots of Street Food

The roots of street food can be traced back through centuries, woven into the fabric of urban life across diverse cultures. Ancient civilizations engaged in street food commerce, with vendors selling a variety of quick, affordable, and flavorful bites to passersby. Whether it was the ancient Greek agora or the vibrant markets of medieval Europe and Asia, street food emerged as a dynamic expression of culinary culture and community.

The Silk Road, the ancient network of trade routes connecting East and West, played a pivotal role in the exchange of spices, ingredients, and cooking techniques. Street food vendors along these routes introduced flavors that transcended borders, shaping the global culinary landscape. The trade of goods and ideas facilitated the spread of diverse street food traditions, creating a tapestry of flavors that continues to evolve and inspire today.

Resurgence in the Modern Era: A Global Culinary Revolution

In recent decades, street food has experienced a remarkable resurgence, propelled by a confluence of factors. Urbanization, a rise in food tourism, and a growing appreciation for authenticity in culinary experiences have all contributed to the revitalization of street food markets worldwide.

Cities like Bangkok, Mexico City, and Mumbai have become celebrated hubs for street food, drawing locals and tourists alike to savor the rich tapestry of flavors offered by street vendors. The resurgence of interest in traditional and regional cuisines has led to a renaissance of street food, with chefs and vendors embracing the challenge of preserving and reimagining age-old recipes.

Social media has played a pivotal role in the global renaissance of street food. Platforms like Instagram and YouTube have transformed humble food stalls into viral sensations, with street food vendors gaining international recognition for their innovative and mouthwatering creations. This digital visibility has not only elevated individual vendors but has also contributed to the broader appreciation of street food as an essential component of global culinary heritage.

Flavors of Diversity: Regional Variations in Street Food

One of the defining features of street food is its ability to reflect the diversity of regional culinary traditions. From the spicy chaat stalls of India to the savory bánh mì carts in Vietnam, street food encapsulates the essence of a culture's flavors, ingredients, and culinary techniques.

Exploring the street food of different regions offers a sensory journey through a kaleidoscope of tastes and aromas. Latin American markets boast vibrant ceviche stalls and the irresistible aroma of grilled arepas. In Southeast Asia, the sizzle of satay skewers and the steam rising from bowls of pho create an immersive culinary experience. Each region's street food tells a unique story, blending historical influences, local ingredients, and a touch of culinary artistry.

Street food vendors often act as culinary ambassadors, preserving traditional recipes while adapting to contemporary tastes. The street food scene in cities like Istanbul, with its succulent kebabs and flavorful mezes, exemplifies how vendors honor their culinary heritage while incorporating modern twists to cater to evolving palates.

Street Food as a Social Phenomenon: Community and Connection

Beyond its culinary delights, street food serves as a social phenomenon, fostering community and connection in the heart of bustling cities and local neighborhoods. In many cultures, street food markets are gathering places where people from all walks of life converge to share a meal, exchange stories, and celebrate the communal spirit of food.

The convivial atmosphere of street food markets transforms dining into a shared experience. From the lively night markets of Taiwan to the aromatic souks of Morocco, street food vendors create a sense of camaraderie among patrons. The communal tables, animated conversations, and the sound of sizzling woks all contribute to an environment where strangers become dining companions, connected by their shared love for authentic and accessible cuisine.

Street food also serves as an economic driver, providing entrepreneurial opportunities for individuals seeking to showcase their culinary skills. In many instances, street food vendors are local artisans, passing down recipes through generations and contributing to the cultural identity of their communities. The economic impact of street food extends beyond the vendors themselves, influencing tourism, creating employment opportunities, and contributing to the overall vibrancy of urban spaces.

Global Influences and Fusions: Culinary Crossroads in the Streets

As street food has gained global popularity, it has become a canvas for culinary experimentation and fusion. In bustling metropolises and cultural crossroads, vendors draw inspiration from diverse culinary traditions, creating innovative and often unexpected flavor combinations.

Cities like Los Angeles and London are renowned for their vibrant food truck scenes, where chefs blend cultural influences to craft unique dishes that defy traditional categorizations. Korean tacos, Thai-infused burgers, and fusion dumplings are just a few examples of how street food becomes a playground for culinary creativity.

This cross-pollination of flavors is not limited to international metropolises. Even in smaller towns, street food vendors draw inspiration from global cuisines, offering a diverse array of options that cater to an increasingly adventurous and culturally curious audience. The fusion of flavors in street food reflects a dynamic interplay between tradition and innovation, resulting in gastronomic creations that capture the imagination and palate.

Innovation and Adaptation: Technology in Street Food

The resurgence of street food is not immune to the influence of technology. While the essence of street food lies in its authenticity and hands-on preparation, technology has facilitated innovations that enhance the street food experience.

Mobile applications and online platforms now allow vendors to reach a wider audience, informing locals and tourists alike about the location, menu, and specialties of street food stalls. This digital visibility helps vendors build a loyal customer base and enables enthusiasts to embark on curated street food tours, discovering hidden gems and culinary delights in unfamiliar neighborhoods.

Food delivery services have also played a role in the evolution of street food. In urban centers, where the pace of life is fast and convenience is paramount, street food vendors partner with delivery platforms to bring their dishes directly to customers' doorsteps. This adaptation ensures that the flavors of street food remain accessible to those with hectic schedules or limited time for traditional dining experiences.

Challenges and Opportunities: Preserving Authenticity in the Face of Commercialization

While the global popularity of street food presents numerous opportunities, it also brings challenges, particularly regarding the preservation of authenticity and the impact of commercialization. As street food gains mainstream recognition, there is a risk of diluting the original flavors and cultural significance that define each dish.

Commercialization can lead to standardization, where vendors prioritize mass appeal over traditional methods and regional nuances. The pressure to cater to a broad audience may result in the simplification or adaptation of recipes, potentially diminishing the authenticity that makes street food unique.

Moreover, as street food becomes a lucrative industry, there is a risk of displacing traditional vendors who lack the resources to compete with larger, more commercial enterprises. Balancing the demand for accessibility and convenience with the need to preserve the grassroots authenticity of street food poses a complex challenge.

Conclusion: Street Food's Enduring Legacy

In conclusion, the resurgence of street food is more than a gastronomic trend; it is a celebration of cultural diversity, culinary heritage, and the enduring legacy of communal dining. From the ancient agora to the bustling night markets of the present day, street food continues to evolve, weaving together the threads of tradition, innovation, and community.

As we navigate the global tapestry of street food, we encounter not just flavors but stories—stories of migration, adaptation, and the vibrant exchange of culinary ideas. Street food's enduring legacy lies in its ability to transcend borders, bringing people together through the universal language of food. Whether savoring a taco from a food truck or relishing the aroma of spices at a bustling market, street food invites us to embark on a journey of discovery, one delicious bite at a time.

Chapter 5: Cultural Significance
Festival Feasts: Discuss food's role in cultural celebrations and festivals.

In the kaleidoscope of global cultures, festivals stand as vibrant tapestries woven with traditions, rituals, and a shared sense of celebration. At the heart of these festivities lies a culinary symphony, where food becomes a pivotal player in orchestrating the sensory experience and cultural significance of each celebration. This exploration delves into the role of festival feasts, examining how they embody cultural identity, foster community bonds, and elevate the spirit of joy during diverse celebrations around the world.

Cultural Threads Woven in Festive Fare

Across continents and cultures, festivals serve as expressions of collective identity, commemorating historical events, religious milestones, or the changing seasons. The cuisine associated with these celebrations acts as a culinary canvas, where traditional recipes, symbolic ingredients, and intricate culinary techniques come together to tell stories of cultural heritage.

In India, the festival of Diwali illuminates homes with the glow of lamps and the fragrance of spices. Diwali feasts are a sensory journey, featuring an array of sweets, savory snacks, and aromatic curries. Each dish carries significance, with sweets symbolizing the sweetness of life, and savory snacks representing the triumph of good over evil. Families come together to prepare these delicacies, passing down recipes through generations and reinforcing a sense of cultural continuity.

Similarly, Chinese New Year marks a time of reunion and renewal, with feasts that emphasize symbolic ingredients and traditional flavors. Dumplings, representing wealth and prosperity, adorn tables, while whole fish symbolizes abundance and the promise of a prosperous year ahead. The act of preparing and sharing these dishes becomes a cultural ritual, connecting generations and reinforcing familial ties.

In Mexico, the Day of the Dead is a poignant celebration that honors departed loved ones. Altars are adorned with marigolds, candles, and photographs, creating a visual feast for the senses. Traditional foods, such as pan de muerto (bread of the dead) and sugar skulls, play a crucial role in the festivities. These offerings are not merely culinary; they serve as gestures of remembrance, love, and the belief that the spirits of the departed return to partake in the joys of life.

The Ritual of Preparation: Culinary Traditions Passed Down Generations

One of the defining aspects of festival feasts is the meticulous preparation and adherence to culinary traditions passed down through generations. The act of cooking during festivals becomes a ritual, a way of honoring ancestors, and a means of preserving cultural identity.

In Italy, the celebration of Christmas Eve, known as La Vigilia, involves a Feast of the Seven Fishes. This tradition, rooted in Catholicism, sees families coming together to enjoy a bountiful seafood feast. The number seven is symbolic, representing the seven sacraments of the Catholic Church. The feast is not just a culinary event; it is a reflection of religious beliefs and the importance of communal sharing.

The Mid-Autumn Festival in China is synonymous with mooncakes, round pastries filled with sweet or savory fillings. Families gather to make and share these mooncakes, symbolizing unity and the fullness of life. The intricate designs on mooncakes often carry cultural motifs and stories, turning the act of baking into a form of edible art that bridges the past and the present.

In Ethiopia, the festival of Timkat, celebrating the baptism of Jesus, involves the preparation of traditional dishes such as injera (fermented flatbread) and doro wat (spicy chicken stew). Families engage in communal cooking, with elders passing on recipes and techniques to younger generations. The preparation and sharing of these dishes strengthen familial bonds and contribute to the continuity of cultural practices.

Symbolism on the Plate: Culinary Customs and Rituals

Festival feasts are rich with symbolism, with each dish carrying layers of meaning that extend beyond the realm of taste. Ingredients, colors, and presentation all contribute to the symbolic language of culinary customs and rituals during cultural celebrations.

In Japan, the cherry blossom season is celebrated with Hanami, where families and friends gather to view cherry blossoms in full bloom. Bento boxes filled with an assortment of dishes, each chosen for its visual and symbolic significance, are a common feature. Pink-hued foods, such as sakura mochi and cherry blossom tea, reflect the ephemeral beauty of the blossoms and the transient nature of life.

During the Jewish festival of Passover, the Seder plate is a focal point laden with symbolic foods representing the story of the Exodus. Items like matzo (unleavened bread), bitter herbs, and charoset (a mixture of fruits and nuts) carry profound meaning, fostering a sense of connection to the ancestral narrative. The act of partaking in these symbolic foods becomes a way of reliving history and reinforcing the cultural identity of the community.

In Nigeria, the festival of New Yam Festival, or Iri Ji Ohuru, is marked by the ceremonial breaking of the kolanut and the offering of the first yams to the gods. The yams are prepared in various dishes, signifying abundance, fertility, and the importance of the harvest. The festival not only celebrates the sustenance provided by the land but also reinforces the cultural ties between the community and the agricultural cycles.

Food Stories: Culinary Narratives Weaved in Festivities

Festival feasts are not only about the flavors on the plate but also about the stories they tell—narratives of cultural resilience, shared history, and the passage of time. These culinary stories become a living archive, preserving the essence of a community's journey and connecting individuals to their cultural roots.

In Greece, the celebration of Easter involves a culinary custom known as Tsoureki, a braided sweet bread. The braids represent the Holy Trinity, and the red-dyed eggs symbolize the blood of Christ. The act of baking Tsoureki is a family affair, with stories of Easter traditions passed down through generations. Sharing the bread during Easter festivities becomes a way of connecting with the past and carrying forward a culinary legacy.

In Brazil, the festival of Festa Junina celebrates the rural life and is marked by traditional foods such as canjica (hominy pudding) and paçoca (peanut candy). These dishes harken back to the country's agrarian roots and are enjoyed during communal festivities that include dance, music, and vibrant costumes. The culinary elements of Festa Junina serve as a bridge between urban and rural cultures, weaving a narrative of Brazil's diverse identity.

In the United States, Thanksgiving is a quintessential festival that revolves around a feast featuring roast turkey, stuffing, and pumpkin pie. The culinary narrative of Thanksgiving is entwined with the country's history, tracing back to the Pilgrims and Native American communities coming together in gratitude. The act of sharing a Thanksgiving meal reflects a national story of unity, gratitude, and the diversity of American cultures.

Festival Feasts as Cultural Bridges: A Culinary Language Beyond Borders

One of the remarkable aspects of festival feasts is their ability to transcend geographical boundaries, serving as cultural bridges that connect people around the world. As global migration and cultural exchange increase, festival foods become a shared language, allowing individuals to celebrate, appreciate, and connect with cultures beyond their own.

In the United Arab Emirates, the festival of Eid al-Fitr is celebrated with an array of festive foods, including dishes like biryani, kebabs, and desserts like baklava. The diverse culinary traditions during Eid reflect the multicultural fabric of the UAE, with flavors influenced by Arab, South Asian, and African cuisines. The act of sharing these dishes during Eid fosters a sense of unity among the diverse communities that call the UAE home.

Similarly, the celebration of the Lunar New Year transcends borders, with Chinese communities worldwide coming together for festive feasts. The iconic reunion dinner, featuring dishes such as fish, dumplings, and longevity noodles, is a global tradition that binds Chinese diaspora communities.

The symbolism and flavors of these dishes serve as a cultural thread, connecting individuals to their heritage regardless of their current geographic location.

Challenges and Evolution: Adapting Festive Feasts in a Changing World

While festival feasts have deep-rooted traditions, they are not immune to the evolving dynamics of the modern world. Changing lifestyles, environmental considerations, and globalization bring forth challenges and adaptations in the way festival feasts are prepared, shared, and experienced.

Urbanization and busy lifestyles have led to shifts in how festival feasts are prepared. Traditional culinary techniques, once passed down through familial traditions, are now adapted to fit contemporary constraints. The convenience of pre-packaged or ready-to-cook ingredients may alter the hands-on, labor-intensive aspects of festival cooking, raising questions about the preservation of culinary heritage in a fast-paced world.

Environmental consciousness is also influencing festival feasts, with communities exploring sustainable and locally sourced ingredients. The impact of climate change and ecological concerns may lead to reevaluations of certain culinary traditions, prompting adaptations that align with a more eco-friendly ethos.

Conclusion: Festival Feasts as Culinary Heritage Keepers

In conclusion, festival feasts emerge as culinary heritage keepers, preserving cultural identities, fostering community bonds, and narrating stories that transcend generations. As we savor the diverse flavors of festival feasts, we partake in a global celebration of cultural richness and the shared human experience. Whether illuminated by the glow of Diwali lamps, the festive lanterns of Mid-Autumn, or the warmth of a Thanksgiving table, festival feasts invite us to embrace the kaleidoscope of cultures that contribute to the global culinary tapestry. In every bite, we find not just sustenance but a connection to the traditions, stories, and shared joy that define the essence of festivals across the world.

Symbolic Ingredients: Highlight ingredients with cultural and symbolic significance.

In the kaleidoscope of global cuisines, certain ingredients transcend their role as mere components of a dish. They become carriers of cultural identity, bearers of tradition, and symbols of profound significance within the communities that cherish them. This exploration delves into the world of symbolic ingredients, examining the stories, rituals, and cultural meanings woven into the very fabric of these culinary elements across diverse cultures.

A Sip of History: Tea in China and Japan

In the ancient tea fields of China and the serene tea gardens of Japan, the leaves of Camellia sinensis are more than just the foundation of a beloved beverage; they are vessels of cultural heritage and spiritual significance. Tea, known as "cha" in China and "matcha" in Japan, has played a pivotal role in shaping social rituals, artistic expressions, and philosophical contemplations for centuries.

In China, the tradition of tea drinking can be traced back to the Tang dynasty (618-907 CE). Tea ceremonies, characterized by intricate gestures and the preparation of various tea varieties, became an integral part of Chinese culture. Beyond its flavorful essence, tea symbolizes harmony, humility, and the appreciation of nature. The act of brewing and sharing tea fosters connections, transcending social hierarchies and embodying the Confucian ideals of respect and interpersonal harmony.

In Japan, the Way of Tea, or "Chanoyu," has deep roots in the Japanese tea ceremony, elevating tea to an art form. Matcha, a powdered green tea, is at the center of this cultural practice. Beyond its earthy taste, matcha represents purity, tranquility, and the ephemeral nature of life. The process of preparing and serving matcha is a choreographed ritual, creating a space for meditation and the appreciation of beauty.

Both in China and Japan, tea is more than a beverage; it is a symbolic journey that transcends taste, inviting individuals to connect with traditions, reflect on the transient nature of existence, and find moments of stillness in a rapidly changing world.

Olive Oil: Liquid Gold and the Mediterranean Tradition

In the sun-drenched landscapes of the Mediterranean, the olive tree stands as an emblem of resilience, abundance, and cultural richness. Olive oil, often referred to as "liquid gold," is not merely a cooking ingredient; it is a cornerstone of Mediterranean identity, a symbol of prosperity, and a thread connecting communities across the region.

The cultivation of olives and the production of olive oil have deep historical roots, dating back to ancient civilizations such as the Greeks and Romans. Olive trees are often passed down through generations, and the process of harvesting olives and pressing them into oil becomes a communal affair, marked by festive gatherings and rituals.

In Mediterranean cultures, olive oil is a fundamental element of culinary traditions, used for cooking, dressing salads, and marinating meats. Its golden hue and rich flavor add depth to dishes while embodying the essence of the land. Beyond the kitchen, olive oil holds cultural significance in religious ceremonies, symbolizing purification, anointing, and the divine connection to the earth.

The olive tree itself is a symbol of endurance and peace. In Greek mythology, the goddess Athena gifted the olive tree to the city of Athens, and the olive branch has since become an international symbol of peace and reconciliation. The cultivation and reverence for olive trees continue to shape the cultural landscape of the Mediterranean, fostering a deep connection between people and the land they inhabit.

Maize: The Sacred Staple of the Americas

In the vast fields of the Americas, maize (corn) stands as a sacred staple that transcends culinary significance, embodying the spiritual and cultural heritage of indigenous communities. Native to the Americas, maize has been cultivated for thousands of years and holds a central place in the traditions, myths, and daily life of diverse cultures, from the Hopi people in the Southwest to the Maya civilization in Mesoamerica.

Maize is more than a source of sustenance; it is a symbol of life, fertility, and the interconnectedness of nature. In many indigenous cultures, the act of planting and harvesting maize is imbued with spiritual rituals, expressing gratitude to the earth and the deities believed to govern the crop.

Among the Hopi people, the cultivation of colorful varieties of maize is a sacred practice intertwined with the cycle of ceremonies known as the "Hopi Year." Different colors of maize represent specific spiritual entities, and the harvest of each variety is accompanied by ceremonies expressing gratitude and seeking blessings for the community.

In Mesoamerican civilizations like the Aztecs and Maya, maize held a central role in creation myths. The Maya believed that humans were created from maize by the gods, highlighting the profound connection between the crop and the origins of life. The Popol Vuh, a sacred text of the K'iche' Maya, describes the hero twins defeating the lords of the underworld and restoring balance to the world, with maize playing a symbolic role in their triumph.

The significance of maize extends beyond rituals to everyday life, with diverse culinary applications in dishes like tortillas, tamales, and pozole. Its versatility in the kitchen mirrors its multifaceted role in the cultural, spiritual, and agricultural realms, reinforcing the deep-rooted connection between indigenous communities and this sacred crop.

Saffron: Threads of Elegance in Persian Cuisine

Amidst the arid landscapes of Iran, the delicate purple flowers of Crocus sativus give birth to saffron, a spice that transcends culinary use to become a symbol of elegance, luxury, and cultural pride. Known as the "red gold" of Iran, saffron threads not only infuse Persian cuisine with a distinct flavor but also carry the weight of historical legacy and artistic inspiration.

The cultivation of saffron in Iran dates back thousands of years, with the spice gaining prominence in the culinary traditions of Persian empires. Saffron's journey from flower to spice is a labor-intensive process, requiring meticulous hand-harvesting and drying of the delicate stigmas. The resulting crimson threads, prized for their vibrant color and aromatic qualities, become an integral part of Persian culinary excellence.

In Persian cuisine, saffron is employed to elevate dishes ranging from rice and stews to desserts. Its inclusion imparts not only a distinct flavor but also a golden hue, symbolizing prosperity and the warmth of hospitality. Saffron-laced rice dishes, such as Persian saffron rice (Zereshk Polo), often grace festive tables, celebrating cultural occasions and connecting generations through shared meals.

Beyond the kitchen, saffron has found its way into Persian art, literature, and rituals. The deep connection between saffron and Persian culture is reflected in classical Persian poetry, where saffron fields become metaphors for beauty and longing. The spice is also used in traditional ceremonies and celebrations, marking moments of joy and significance in the lives of Iranians.

Chilies: Spice and Spirit in Mexican Cuisine

In the vibrant tapestry of Mexican cuisine, the humble chili pepper emerges as a fiery symbol of flavor, tradition, and spiritual significance. Whether in the form of jalapeños, poblanos, or the iconic red chili, these peppers not only lend heat to dishes but also carry cultural stories, indigenous legacies, and a connection to the land.

Chilies have been cultivated in the Americas for thousands of years, with evidence of their use dating back to ancient civilizations like the Aztecs and Maya. The indigenous peoples of Mesoamerica not only incorporated chilies into their culinary practices but also recognized their medicinal and spiritual properties.

In contemporary Mexican cuisine, chilies are omnipresent, adding depth and complexity to dishes. From the smoky heat of chipotle to the earthy richness of ancho, each variety contributes a unique flavor profile. Chilies are not just ingredients; they are cultural markers, reflecting the diverse ecosystems of Mexico and the culinary ingenuity of its people.

The symbolism of chilies extends beyond the kitchen to indigenous rituals and beliefs. In many indigenous cultures, chilies are considered sacred plants with protective qualities. The act of planting and harvesting chilies is often accompanied by rituals expressing gratitude to the earth and seeking blessings for a bountiful harvest.

In Mexican folklore, the legend of La Llorona (The Weeping Woman) is intertwined with the symbolism of chilies. La Llorona, a ghostly figure said to weep for her lost children, is often depicted carrying chilies. The inclusion of chilies in this folklore reflects their cultural importance and the connection between sustenance, grief, and the cyclical nature of life.

Conclusion: Culinary Alchemy of Symbolic Ingredients

In conclusion, the exploration of symbolic ingredients unravels the culinary alchemy that transforms ordinary elements into cultural treasures. From the tea fields of China to the olive groves of the Mediterranean, from the maize fields of the Americas to the saffron fields of Iran, and from the chili-laden kitchens of Mexico to countless kitchens around the world, symbolic ingredients weave narratives that connect individuals to their roots, histories, and the collective human experience.

These ingredients, infused with cultural meanings and culinary prowess, transcend geographical boundaries, offering a taste of the rich tapestry of human heritage. As we savor dishes seasoned with symbolic ingredients, we partake in a communion with the past, present, and future—a gastronomic journey that goes beyond the palate, inviting us to appreciate the stories, traditions, and cultural wisdom encapsulated in each flavorful thread.

Culinary Customs: Explore unique culinary rituals and traditions worldwide.

In the vast tapestry of global cultures, culinary customs emerge as sacred threads, weaving intricate patterns of tradition, community, and symbolism. Beyond the realm of recipes and ingredients, these customs are the rhythmic heartbeat of societies, shaping the way people gather, celebrate, and pass down their heritage. This exploration delves into the diverse culinary customs that span continents, revealing the rich tapestry of rituals that accompany the act of sharing a meal.

The Japanese Tea Ceremony: An Ode to Harmony

In the serene realms of Japan, the Way of Tea, or "Chanoyu," unfolds as a centuries-old cultural practice that extends far beyond the simple act of drinking tea. Rooted in Zen Buddhism, this intricate ritual represents a harmonious fusion of aesthetics, philosophy, and social interaction.

The Japanese tea ceremony is an immersive experience that takes place in a purpose-built tea room, often nestled in a tranquil garden. The host, adorned in traditional attire, meticulously prepares and serves matcha, a powdered green tea, to a small group of guests. Every gesture, from the precise movements in whisking the tea to the choreographed placement of utensils, carries profound meaning.

At its core, the tea ceremony embodies principles such as harmony (wa), respect (kei), purity (sei), and tranquility (jaku). Beyond the flavors of the tea itself, participants engage in a meditative journey, fostering a sense of connection with one another and the surrounding natural elements. The ceremony becomes a spiritual pause, inviting contemplation and the appreciation of beauty in simplicity.

The Way of Tea is not just a customary routine; it is a cultural transmission, often passed down through generations within families or shared among close-knit communities. The utensils used in the ceremony, such as the tea bowl and bamboo whisk, carry historical significance and may be treasured heirlooms. The act of partaking in a tea ceremony transcends the temporal boundaries of the moment, connecting participants to the timeless elegance of Japanese culture.

Injera and the Ethiopian Communal Feast

In the highlands of Ethiopia, the communal feast, known as "messob," emerges as a vibrant expression of hospitality, community, and the rich cultural tapestry of the country. At the heart of this culinary custom is injera, a spongy flatbread with a slightly tangy flavor, made from fermented teff flour.

The communal feast is a social event that extends beyond immediate family to include neighbors, friends, and sometimes even strangers. A large round table, known as a "messob," serves as the centerpiece for the feast. Injera, laid out in a circular pattern, becomes both the plate and the utensil for scooping up various stews, known as "wats," which are arranged in the center.

Participating in the communal feast is an inclusive and interactive experience. Guests sit around the messob, tearing off pieces of injera to scoop up the flavorful wats. The act of sharing food from a common plate symbolizes unity, and the communal setting fosters a sense of connection among participants.

The injera itself holds cultural and spiritual significance. Beyond its role as a culinary staple, injera is a symbol of sustenance, community, and the interconnectedness of

Ethiopian society. The process of making injera is often a shared activity, with family members or neighbors coming together to prepare the fermented batter and cook the flatbread on a large, round griddle.

This culinary custom also extends to cultural celebrations and religious ceremonies, where the communal feast becomes a manifestation of joy, generosity, and the communal spirit. Injera, with its unique texture and taste, becomes a vessel for the flavors of Ethiopia and a medium through which cultural identity is both preserved and shared.

The Italian Sunday Dinner: A Culinary Family Affair

In the sun-drenched landscapes of Italy, the Sunday dinner unfolds as more than a mere meal; it is a cherished tradition that brings families together, celebrating the essence of la dolce vita (the sweet life). Rooted in a culture that places importance on food, family, and togetherness, the Sunday dinner is a weekly ritual that honors culinary heritage and reinforces the bonds of kinship.

The preparation of the Sunday dinner often begins early in the morning, with family members contributing to the feast. Pasta, with its myriad shapes and textures, is a quintessential element, and the process of making fresh pasta becomes a communal activity. The aroma of simmering sauces, the kneading of dough, and the clatter of pots and pans create a symphony that resonates throughout the household.

As the day progresses, the extended family gathers around a long table laden with an array of dishes. The Sunday dinner is not just about the food; it is a time for laughter, storytelling, and the reaffirmation of familial bonds. The meal unfolds slowly, with multiple courses, each representing a journey through the diverse culinary regions of Italy.

The Sunday dinner is a testament to the Italian philosophy of savoring life's pleasures. It is a moment to pause, appreciate the abundance of the land, and revel in the joy of shared company. Generations come together during these gatherings, with grandparents passing down traditional recipes, parents sharing anecdotes of their youth, and children learning the art of crafting the perfect risotto or shaping handmade gnocchi.

The Sunday dinner is a culinary custom that transcends the flavors on the plate; it encapsulates the warmth of familial love, the joy of storytelling, and the continuity of cultural identity. Whether gathered around a rustic farmhouse table in Tuscany or in a bustling apartment in Rome, the Sunday dinner embodies the timeless spirit of Italian gastronomy and the importance of savoring life's simple pleasures.

The Ritual of Argentine Asado: Grilling with Passion

In the vast landscapes of Argentina, the tradition of asado, or barbecue, stands as a culinary custom that goes beyond mere cooking; it is a cultural phenomenon that encapsulates the passion, sociality, and distinctive flavors of Argentine cuisine.

Asado is not just a meal; it is a ritual, an event that brings friends and family together in a celebration of fire, meat, and camaraderie. The process begins with the selection of quality meat, often beef, and the preparation of the grill, known as a parrilla. As the flames flicker and the coals glow, the air becomes infused with the enticing aroma of grilling meat.

The act of grilling is an art form, with each cut of meat receiving meticulous attention. Various cuts, such as ribs, flank steaks, and sausages, are arranged on the parrilla, each requiring a different cooking time and technique. Asado is not rushed; it is a slow, deliberate process that allows participants to savor the anticipation and the company of those around them.

The social aspect of asado is integral to its essence. Friends and family gather around the grill, engaging in lively conversations, sharing stories, and sipping on mate, a traditional Argentine herbal tea. The atmosphere is relaxed, fostering a sense of community and the enjoyment of the present moment.

Asado also carries historical and cultural significance in Argentina. The tradition of grilling meat over an open flame dates back to the indigenous peoples of the region, and it was further shaped by the arrival of European immigrants, particularly those from Italy and Spain. Over time, asado became a symbol of national identity, reflecting the vast pampas, the gaucho lifestyle, and the abundance of high-quality Argentine beef.

Participating in an asado is not just about the consumption of grilled meat; it is an immersive experience that connects individuals to the land, the cultural heritage, and the convivial spirit of Argentina. As the embers glow and the laughter echoes under the vast South American sky, the ritual of asado becomes a timeless celebration of life, friendship, and the flavors that define Argentine gastronomy.

Conclusion: Threads of Unity in Culinary Customs

In conclusion, the exploration of culinary customs unravels the threads of unity that bind communities together through shared rituals and traditions. From the meditative ceremonies of the Japanese tea room to the vibrant messob feasts of Ethiopia, from the convivial Sunday dinners of Italy to the passionate rituals of Argentine asado, each culinary custom reflects the values, histories, and identities of the cultures that practice them.

Culinary customs serve as a universal language, transcending linguistic barriers and connecting individuals on a profound level. They are not merely activities related to food; they are expressions of cultural pride, familial love, and the human need for connection. As we delve into these diverse culinary customs, we embark on a global journey that goes beyond the plate, inviting us to savor the rich tapestry of human experiences, one shared meal at a time.

Food Stories: Share stories and legends related to cultural dishes.

In the kaleidoscope of global cuisines, dishes are more than just combinations of ingredients; they are vessels of stories, legends, and cultural narratives. Behind each bite lies a tale of heritage, identity, and the human experience. This exploration delves into the rich tapestry of food stories, unraveling the narratives woven into cultural dishes across diverse corners of the world.

Sushi and the Legend of Hanaya Yohei: Crafting Edo-Mae Perfection

In the bustling streets of Edo-period Tokyo, a culinary legend emerged that would forever shape the world of sushi. The story centers around Hanaya Yohei, a visionary chef who transformed humble street food into an art form, laying the foundation for what we now know as Edo-mae sushi.

During the early 19th century, Tokyo was a vibrant hub of commerce, and street vendors thrived in the energetic atmosphere. Hanaya Yohei, a quick-witted and innovative chef, sought to elevate the simple combination of vinegared rice and fresh fish into a culinary masterpiece. His breakthrough came when he started using bite-sized portions of sushi, allowing customers to enjoy a variety of flavors in one sitting.

Despite initial skepticism, Hanaya's approach gained popularity, and he became a culinary sensation. The legend of Hanaya Yohei and his innovative sushi spread throughout Edo and beyond, transforming sushi from a portable snack to a revered dining experience. Today, Edo-mae sushi, characterized by precision, freshness, and a respect for seasonal ingredients, stands as a testament to Hanaya's pioneering spirit and the enduring legacy of his culinary innovation.

Biryani and the Romance of Mumtaz Mahal: A Culinary Love Story

In the heart of Mughal India, the origins of biryani are intertwined with the grandeur of the Mughal Empire and the enduring love between Shah Jahan and Mumtaz Mahal. Legend has it that Mumtaz, the beloved wife of the emperor, visited the military barracks to witness the lives of the soldiers. Struck by the sight of malnourished troops, she urged the royal chefs to create a nutritious and flavorful dish that could nourish the soldiers.

The result was biryani, a fragrant and richly spiced rice dish layered with succulent meats. The use of aromatic spices and slow-cooking techniques not only produced a dish that satisfied the nutritional needs of the soldiers but also captivated the palates of the royal court. The dish was named after Mumtaz, symbolizing the union of flavors and the love that inspired its creation.

Today, biryani stands as a culinary masterpiece, celebrated across the Indian subcontinent and beyond. The dish reflects the cultural synthesis of Mughal influences with regional flavors, embodying the spirit of a bygone era and the enduring romance between Shah Jahan and Mumtaz Mahal. Each spoonful of biryani carries with it the echoes of a love story that transcended time and left an indelible mark on the world of gastronomy.

Tamales and the Spirit of Inti Raymi: An Inca Culinary Celebration

In the Andean highlands, the tradition of making tamales is deeply rooted in the ancient Inca festival of Inti Raymi, a celebration of the sun god. The legend traces back to a time when the Inca people offered tamales as a sacred offering to Inti, expressing gratitude for the sun's warmth and life-giving energy.

According to the myth, the first tamales were crafted from corn, a sacred crop believed to be a gift from the gods. The Inca people, recognizing the importance of corn in their sustenance, created tamales as a symbolic gesture of reciprocity with the divine. The preparation of tamales became a communal affair, with families gathering to share the labor and partake in the spiritual significance of the process.

The festival of Inti Raymi, marked by the winter solstice, is a time of abundance and reverence for the cycles of nature. Tamales, with their corn husk wrappings and diverse fillings, became a culinary representation of the harmonious relationship between the Inca people and the natural world. Today, the tradition of making tamales during Inti Raymi endures, serving as a link to the ancient rituals of the Inca civilization and a celebration of the interconnectedness of life.

Peking Duck and the Imperial Banquets: A Culinary Spectacle

In the heart of imperial China, the legend of Peking duck unfolds as a culinary spectacle fit for royalty. The story traces back to the Ming Dynasty, where the imperial kitchens perfected the art of roasting duck to create a dish that not only delighted the senses but also captivated the eyes.

Legend has it that the process of preparing Peking duck was a closely guarded secret within the imperial kitchens. The ducks were seasoned, air-dried, and roasted to perfection, resulting in a crispy, golden skin and tender meat. The presentation of the dish became an integral part of the culinary experience, with skilled chefs slicing the duck tableside into thin, glistening strips.

Peking duck became a centerpiece of imperial banquets, a symbol of opulence, and a dish fit for emperors. The culinary legend of Peking duck spread beyond the imperial court, captivating the palates of commoners and travelers alike. Today, Peking duck stands as a culinary icon, celebrated for its meticulous preparation, rich flavors, and the visual artistry of its presentation—a testament to the enduring legacy of the imperial kitchens and their culinary innovations.

Gumbo and the Melting Pot of Louisiana: A Culinary Fusion

In the melting pot of Louisiana, the legend of gumbo unfolds as a culinary fusion that reflects the diverse cultural influences of the region. Rooted in West African, French, Spanish, and Indigenous culinary traditions, gumbo is a hearty stew that brings together a medley of ingredients to create a dish that transcends cultural boundaries.

The legend of gumbo traces back to the colonial era, where enslaved West Africans combined okra—a key ingredient in gumbo—with local shellfish and game. The French and Spanish settlers added their culinary contributions, introducing roux as a thickening agent and incorporating ingredients like tomatoes and bell peppers. The result was a flavorful and complex stew that became a culinary symbol of Louisiana's cultural diversity.

Gumbo became a communal dish, often prepared during festive gatherings and celebrations. The act of making gumbo became a social event, with family and community members contributing their unique ingredients and techniques. The dish not only embodies the historical roots of Louisiana but also serves as a testament to the resilience and creativity of the people who shaped its culinary landscape.

Conclusion: Tasting the Legends

In conclusion, the exploration of food stories unveils the rich tapestry of legends and narratives woven into cultural dishes. From the precision of Edo-mae sushi to the romance of biryani, from the sacred tamales of Inti Raymi to the imperial spectacle of Peking duck, and from the diverse influences of Louisiana gumbo to the enduring love story behind each bite of biryani, these legends transcend the boundaries of time and place.

Culinary tales are not only about the ingredients on the plate; they are about the people, cultures, and histories that converge in the act of sharing a meal. As we savor these legendary dishes, we partake in a communion with the past, present, and future—a gastronomic journey that invites us to appreciate the stories, traditions, and cultural wisdom encapsulated in each flavorful bite.

Chapter 6: Farm-to-Table Movements
Sustainable Origins: Explore the farm-to-table movement and sustainable practices.

In the evolving landscape of global gastronomy, the farm-to-table movement has emerged as a paradigm shift, redefining the way we think about food. This exploration delves into the roots of the farm-to-table movement, its underlying principles, and the sustainable practices that have become integral to reshaping the culinary narrative.

Cultivating Conscious Connections: The Essence of Farm-to-Table

At the heart of the farm-to-table movement lies a fundamental shift in the way we source, prepare, and consume food. The movement champions the idea of shortening the distance between producers and consumers, fostering a direct and conscious connection between the farm and the table.

Farm-to-table is not merely a culinary trend but a philosophy that emphasizes transparency, sustainability, and a return to the roots of agriculture. By prioritizing local, seasonal, and responsibly sourced ingredients, the movement seeks to minimize the environmental impact of food production while supporting local farmers and communities.

The essence of farm-to-table lies in understanding the journey of food from the soil to the plate. This awareness encourages consumers to appreciate the seasonal nuances of ingredients, celebrate biodiversity, and acknowledge the efforts of farmers who cultivate the land with care and respect for natural ecosystems.

The Roots of the Movement: A Back-to-Basics Approach

The farm-to-table movement traces its origins to a back-to-basics approach, challenging the industrialized and globalized food systems that dominated the latter part of the 20th century. As concerns about the environmental, social, and health impacts of conventional agriculture grew, a countermovement emerged, advocating for a return to traditional, sustainable farming practices.

One of the pioneers of the farm-to-table movement is chef and activist Alice Waters, whose iconic restaurant, Chez Panisse, in Berkeley, California, became a beacon for locally sourced, seasonal cuisine. Waters's vision was grounded in the belief that food should be fresh, flavorful, and reflective of the surrounding landscape. Her commitment to working directly with local farmers set a precedent that inspired a generation of chefs and consumers to prioritize the quality and origin of their ingredients.

As the movement gained momentum, farmers' markets became key conduits for connecting producers with consumers. These vibrant marketplaces not only provided a platform for farmers to showcase their products but also became community hubs, fostering a sense of shared values and a commitment to sustainable, locally driven food systems.

Sustainability Beyond the Plate: Environmental Impact and Conservation

One of the core tenets of the farm-to-table movement is its commitment to environmental sustainability. Conventional agriculture practices, marked by monoculture, heavy pesticide use, and long-distance transportation, contribute significantly to ecological degradation and climate change. In contrast, the farm-to-table movement embraces practices that prioritize the health of the planet.

Regenerative agriculture, a key component of sustainable farming, focuses on improving soil health, enhancing biodiversity, and sequestering carbon. By implementing techniques such as cover cropping, crop rotation, and agroforestry, regenerative farmers not only produce high-quality, nutrient-dense food but also contribute to the restoration of ecosystems.

The movement also places a strong emphasis on reducing food miles—the distance food travels from the farm to the consumer. By sourcing ingredients locally, the carbon footprint associated with transportation is minimized, mitigating the environmental impact of the food supply chain. This localized approach not only supports regional economies but also fosters a sense of community resilience.

Nurturing Relationships: Farmers, Chefs, and Community Collaboration

Central to the success of the farm-to-table movement is the cultivation of collaborative relationships among farmers, chefs, and the community. This interconnected network fosters a sense of shared responsibility for the food we consume and the impact it has on the environment.

Farmers, often the unsung heroes of the movement, play a pivotal role in shaping the culinary landscape. Through direct relationships with chefs, they can grow crops tailored to local tastes and seasonal availability. This personalized approach not only ensures the freshness and quality of ingredients but also creates a dynamic feedback loop between the farm and the kitchen.

Chefs, in turn, become advocates for sustainable practices and ambassadors of local flavors. Their role extends beyond the kitchen to the forefront of educating consumers about the importance of supporting local agriculture and making informed choices about the food they eat. By featuring farmers' stories on menus and showcasing the diversity of locally sourced ingredients, chefs elevate the farm-to-table experience to a narrative of shared values and appreciation for the land.

Community collaboration is a cornerstone of the farm-to-table movement, with farmers' markets, community-supported agriculture (CSA) programs, and local food events serving as platforms for engagement. These initiatives not only connect consumers with the source of their food but also create spaces for dialogue, education, and the celebration of regional culinary identities.

Challenges and Solutions: Navigating the Complexities of Sustainability

While the farm-to-table movement has made significant strides in promoting sustainability, it is not without its challenges. The complexities of modern food systems, economic pressures, and the need for scalability present hurdles that farmers, chefs, and advocates must navigate to ensure the movement's continued success.

One challenge is the economic viability of small-scale, local agriculture. Industrialized agriculture, with its economies of scale, often outcompetes smaller operations in terms of pricing. To address this, consumers play a crucial role in supporting local farmers through their purchasing choices. By prioritizing quality over quantity and understanding the true cost of sustainably produced food, consumers contribute to the economic resilience of local food systems.

Another challenge is the need for increased awareness and education about sustainable practices. Both consumers and producers benefit from understanding the ecological impact of different farming methods and the importance of biodiversity in preserving ecosystems. Initiatives such as farm tours, educational workshops, and collaboration with schools can enhance public awareness and empower individuals to make informed choices.

Technological innovations also play a role in overcoming challenges associated with sustainability. Precision agriculture, for example, leverages data and technology to optimize farming practices, reducing inputs and minimizing environmental impact. By embracing innovative solutions that align with sustainable principles, farmers can enhance efficiency while preserving natural resources.

Global Perspectives: Farm-to-Table Movements Around the World

While the farm-to-table movement has its roots in the United States, similar initiatives have gained traction worldwide. Each region brings its unique cultural, agricultural, and culinary context to the concept of sourcing locally and sustainably.

In Europe, the "terroir" movement emphasizes the importance of a sense of place in food production. Originating in France, the term "terroir" encompasses the environmental factors, including soil, climate, and topography, that influence the flavor and character of food and beverages. This movement aligns with the farm-to-table ethos, promoting the connection between regional identity and culinary excellence.

In Scandinavia, the "New Nordic Cuisine" movement places a strong emphasis on seasonal, local ingredients and traditional culinary techniques. Spearheaded by chefs like René Redzepi of Noma in Copenhagen, this movement has elevated Nordic ingredients and redefined the global perception of Nordic gastronomy.

In Japan, the "Satoyama" and "Satoumi" movements focus on the sustainable management of rural landscapes and coastal environments, respectively. These movements highlight the interconnectedness of human communities and ecosystems, promoting practices that balance agricultural productivity with environmental conservation.

In Latin America, initiatives such as "Campesino a Campesino" in Mexico and the "Pole to Pole" movement in Argentina aim to strengthen local food systems and empower small-scale farmers. These movements emphasize the cultural importance of traditional agricultural practices and seek to preserve biodiversity while promoting community resilience.

Beyond Cuisine: The Social Impact of Farm-to-Table

The farm-to-table movement extends beyond the realm of cuisine, making significant contributions to social, economic, and health-related aspects of communities. By championing sustainable practices, fostering local economies, and prioritizing the well-being of both consumers and producers, the movement serves as a catalyst for positive change.

Economic Resilience and Local Empowerment

One of the notable outcomes of the farm-to-table movement is its impact on local economies and the empowerment of small-scale farmers. By creating direct connections between farmers and consumers, the movement bypasses traditional distribution channels that often marginalize producers. This direct-to-consumer model allows farmers to receive fair compensation for their products, contributing to the economic resilience of local agricultural communities.

In addition to economic benefits, the movement empowers local farmers by providing a platform for them to share their stories, expertise, and heritage. Farmers become active participants in shaping culinary narratives, and their knowledge of traditional farming practices contributes to the preservation of agricultural biodiversity and cultural heritage.

Community Health and Well-Being

The farm-to-table movement's emphasis on fresh, seasonal, and locally sourced ingredients has significant implications for public health and well-being. Access to nutrient-dense foods, free from the additives and preservatives commonly found in processed products, contributes to healthier diets and lifestyles.

Farmers' markets, community-supported agriculture programs, and local food events serve as avenues for promoting nutritional education and fostering a deeper understanding of the connection between diet and well-being. By prioritizing diverse, whole foods, the movement encourages a shift away from reliance on highly processed and industrially produced foods, contributing to the prevention of diet-related health issues.

Environmental Stewardship and Conservation

At its core, the farm-to-table movement is a commitment to environmental stewardship and the conservation of natural resources. Sustainable farming practices, such as regenerative agriculture, contribute to soil health, biodiversity, and carbon sequestration. By prioritizing local sourcing and reducing food miles, the movement minimizes the carbon footprint associated with food production and transportation.

The conservation of heirloom and indigenous crop varieties is another aspect of the movement's environmental impact. As farmers prioritize the cultivation of traditional and locally adapted crops, they contribute to the preservation of agricultural diversity, which is essential for the resilience of ecosystems and the adaptation to changing climatic conditions.

Educational Initiatives and Food Literacy

Educational initiatives play a crucial role in the farm-to-table movement, fostering food literacy and empowering consumers to make informed choices about the food they eat. By connecting people with the source of their food through farm tours, cooking classes, and educational workshops, the movement encourages a deeper understanding of the complexities of the food system.

Food literacy encompasses knowledge about where food comes from, how it is produced, and the impact of different agricultural practices on the environment. As consumers become more informed, they are better equipped to make choices aligned with their values, whether it be supporting local farmers, choosing organic products, or advocating for sustainable agricultural policies.

Challenges and Opportunities in the Global Context

While the farm-to-table movement has made significant strides in promoting sustainable practices, its global expansion is not without challenges. Different regions face unique socio-economic, cultural, and environmental considerations that influence the adoption and success of farm-to-table initiatives.

In densely populated urban areas, for example, the availability of space for local agriculture and the logistics of supplying fresh produce to a large population pose challenges. However, innovative solutions such as rooftop gardens, urban agriculture, and community-supported agriculture programs address these challenges by bringing food production closer to urban centers.

In economically marginalized regions, the affordability of sustainably produced food is a critical consideration. The farm-to-table movement often faces the perception that locally sourced and organic products are more expensive than conventionally produced alternatives. Addressing this challenge requires a combination of public awareness, policy support, and efforts to make sustainably produced food more economically accessible.

Future Pathways: Innovations and Collaborations

As the farm-to-table movement continues to evolve, innovations and collaborations are key to overcoming existing challenges and realizing its full potential. A range of initiatives and practices are shaping the future of sustainable gastronomy and reinforcing the interconnectedness between producers, consumers, and the planet.

Technological Innovations in Agriculture

Advancements in agricultural technology play a pivotal role in enhancing the sustainability of farming practices. Precision agriculture, which utilizes data and technology to optimize crop management, resource use, and environmental impact, offers opportunities to increase efficiency while minimizing inputs.

Drones, satellite imaging, and sensor technologies provide farmers with real-time data on soil health, moisture levels, and crop conditions. This information enables precise decision-making, allowing farmers to reduce water and pesticide usage, optimize planting and harvesting times, and minimize environmental impact.

In addition to precision agriculture, the use of vertical farming and hydroponics represents innovative approaches to urban agriculture. These methods allow for year-round cultivation in controlled environments, maximizing space efficiency and reducing the environmental footprint associated with traditional farming.

Blockchain and Transparent Supply Chains

Blockchain technology is increasingly being explored as a tool to enhance transparency and traceability in food supply chains. By creating secure, decentralized ledgers of transactions, blockchain allows for the recording of every step in the production, processing, and distribution of food products.

For consumers, blockchain provides a means to trace the origin of their food, ensuring that it has been produced ethically, sustainably, and in accordance with their values. This level of transparency fosters trust between producers and consumers, creating a more informed and conscientious food system.

Collaborations Between Culinary and Agricultural Sectors

Collaborations between chefs and farmers are essential for the continued success of the farm-to-table movement. These partnerships go beyond transactional relationships and involve chefs working closely with farmers to co-create menus, experiment with heirloom varieties, and explore innovative culinary techniques.

Initiatives such as farm dinners, where chefs prepare meals using locally sourced ingredients at the farm itself, bridge the gap between the agricultural and culinary worlds. These events provide opportunities for consumers to connect with the source of their food, meet the farmers, and gain a deeper appreciation for the complexities of sustainable agriculture.

Policy Advocacy and Sustainable Agriculture

Policy support is crucial for advancing sustainable agriculture and the farm-to-table movement. Advocacy for policies that prioritize local sourcing, sustainable farming practices, and equitable access to resources contributes to creating an enabling environment for the movement to thrive.

Government incentives, subsidies, and regulations that support small-scale farmers, regenerative agriculture, and sustainable food production practices play a pivotal role in shaping the agricultural landscape. Collaborative efforts between policymakers, farmers, chefs, and consumers can lead to the development of frameworks that prioritize environmental stewardship, social equity, and economic resilience.

Educational Programs and Culinary Training

Integrating sustainable agriculture and farm-to-table principles into culinary education is essential for shaping the next generation of chefs and culinary professionals. Culinary schools can play a proactive role in educating students about the environmental and social impact of food choices, sourcing practices, and the principles of sustainability.

Educational programs that emphasize the connection between agriculture and cuisine empower chefs to make informed decisions in their culinary practices. This awareness extends to menu planning, sourcing decisions, waste reduction strategies, and the integration of seasonal and locally available ingredients into culinary creations.

The Global Impact of Local Choices

The farm-to-table movement exemplifies how individual choices at the local level can have a global impact. By choosing locally sourced and sustainably produced food, consumers contribute to a more resilient, equitable, and environmentally conscious food system.

The global impact of local choices extends beyond culinary preferences to influence the broader discourse on sustainability, climate change, and the future of food. As individuals, communities, and businesses align their values with their consumption patterns, they become active participants in a movement that transcends borders and fosters a collective commitment to the well-being of the planet and its inhabitants.

Conclusion: Cultivating Culinary Consciousness

In conclusion, the exploration of sustainable origins within the farm-to-table movement reveals a profound shift in our relationship with food—a shift that encompasses ecological stewardship, community empowerment, and the celebration of culinary diversity. By delving into the essence of farm-to-table, we uncover not only a movement but a philosophy—a philosophy that recognizes the interconnectedness of the choices we make at the table with the health of the planet and the well-being of communities.

The journey from the farm to the table becomes a narrative of conscious choices, where every ingredient tells a story of ethical cultivation, responsible stewardship, and a commitment to preserving the richness of our culinary heritage. As we savor the flavors of sustainably sourced meals, we partake in a collective act of culinary consciousness—a celebration of the intricate web that connects farmers, chefs, consumers, and the earth in a harmonious dance of flavors and values.

The farm-to-table movement invites us to consider not only the taste on our plates but also the impact of our choices on the world around us. As we cultivate a deeper understanding of the origins of our food, we empower ourselves to make choices that resonate with our values, contributing to a global tapestry of sustainable gastronomy—a tapestry that continues to unfold with each mindful, delicious bite.

Community Connection: Discuss how this movement fosters community connections.

In the tapestry of sustainable gastronomy, the farm-to-table movement weaves a thread of community connection that extends far beyond the boundaries of individual plates. At its core, this movement transcends the transactional relationship between producers and consumers, fostering a sense of shared responsibility, mutual support, and vibrant interconnectedness within communities.

Culinary Collaboration: Farmers, Chefs, and Consumers Unite

At the heart of the farm-to-table movement is a collaborative spirit that unites farmers, chefs, and consumers in a shared appreciation for locally sourced, seasonal ingredients. This collaborative approach not only transforms the way we think about food but also redefines the relationships within the culinary ecosystem.

Farmers, often the unsung heroes of the movement, take center stage as active contributors to the culinary narrative. Their dedication to sustainable farming practices, coupled with a commitment to cultivating diverse and high-quality produce, becomes a source of inspiration for chefs seeking to craft menus that reflect the terroir of their regions.

Chefs, in turn, become curators of local flavors, crafting menus that showcase the diversity and freshness of seasonal ingredients. The direct relationships forged between farmers and chefs lead to dynamic collaborations, where menus evolve with the changing seasons, creating a culinary experience that resonates with the rhythms of nature.

For consumers, this culinary collaboration translates into a richer and more meaningful dining experience. The transparency inherent in the farm-to-table movement allows individuals to trace the journey of their food from the fields to their plates. This connection sparks a deeper appreciation for the effort, care, and expertise invested by both farmers and chefs in delivering a culinary experience that is not only delicious but also ethically and sustainably sourced.

Farmers' Markets as Community Hubs

Farmers' markets emerge as vibrant hubs of community connection within the farm-to-table movement. Beyond being spaces for the exchange of goods, these markets become gathering places where farmers and consumers engage in conversations, share stories, and forge connections that extend beyond the transactional.

The direct interaction between farmers and consumers at these markets fosters a sense of trust and accountability. Consumers gain insights into the growing practices, harvesting techniques, and stories behind the produce they purchase. This transparency builds a foundation of trust, as consumers can confidently make choices aligned with their values, supporting local agriculture and sustainable practices.

Farmers, in turn, become more than suppliers—they become storytellers, sharing the narratives of their farms, the challenges they overcome, and the pride they take in producing food that nourishes the community. These personal connections create a shared sense of responsibility for the well-being of the land, the community, and the future of sustainable agriculture.

The communal atmosphere of farmers' markets extends beyond the exchange of goods to include social interactions, culinary demonstrations, and educational initiatives. Cooking demonstrations featuring local chefs, workshops on sustainable living, and activities for children transform farmers' markets into lively community events that celebrate the intersection of food, culture, and shared values.

Community-Supported Agriculture (CSA): Shared Responsibility and Bounty

Community-Supported Agriculture (CSA) programs represent a pillar of community connection within the farm-to-table movement. In a CSA model, individuals or families become shareholders in a local farm, receiving a regular share of the harvest throughout the growing season. This direct relationship between farmers and consumers forms a cooperative bond built on shared responsibility and shared bounty.

Participating in a CSA program goes beyond a mere economic transaction; it becomes a commitment to the well-being of the farm and the community. Shareholders share in the risks and rewards of farming, understanding that factors such as weather, pests, and other unforeseen challenges can impact the harvest. This shared risk fosters a deeper connection to the agricultural rhythms that shape the food on their tables.

The regular delivery of seasonal produce introduces an element of culinary adventure for CSA members. Each share becomes a curated selection of the freshest and most diverse offerings from the farm, inspiring creativity in the kitchen and encouraging individuals to explore new recipes and cooking techniques.

CSA programs often incorporate community events such as farm tours, volunteer days, and harvest celebrations. These gatherings create opportunities for shareholders to visit the farms, connect with the farmers, and forge friendships with fellow members. The sense of belonging and shared purpose that emerges from CSA participation reinforces the notion that the farm is not just a supplier of food but an integral part of a larger community.

Restaurants as Community Spaces

Within the farm-to-table movement, restaurants become more than places to dine; they transform into community spaces that embody the ethos of local sourcing, sustainability, and collaboration. Chefs, as community stewards, take on roles beyond culinary creators—they become advocates for regional agriculture, educators, and catalysts for positive change.

Restaurants that embrace the farm-to-table philosophy often extend their commitment to community connection beyond their menus. Collaborations with local artisans, artists, and musicians infuse the dining experience with a sense of place and cultural richness. This integration of various creative elements transforms restaurants into dynamic hubs where the community can gather, celebrate, and connect.

Chef-led initiatives, such as themed dinners, spotlight local producers and artisans, creating platforms for these community members to share their stories with a broader audience. The integration of storytelling into the dining experience transforms restaurants into spaces that celebrate the interconnected narratives of the local food ecosystem.

Moreover, restaurants actively engage in educational outreach, hosting events such as cooking classes, workshops, and tastings. These initiatives not only empower consumers with culinary skills but also deepen their understanding of the farm-to-table movement, sustainable practices, and the importance of supporting local agriculture.

Educational Initiatives: Nourishing Minds and Palates

Educational initiatives emerge as powerful tools for fostering community connection within the farm-to-table movement. By nourishing minds along with palates, these initiatives empower individuals with the knowledge and skills to make informed choices about the food they eat, while also cultivating a deeper appreciation for the interconnected web of agriculture, culture, and sustainability.

School gardens represent one avenue for introducing children to the principles of farm-to-table living. These gardens become living classrooms where students learn about the life cycles of plants, the importance of soil health, and the joy of growing and harvesting their own food. The experience extends beyond gardening to include lessons in nutrition, environmental stewardship, and the cultural significance of diverse foods.

Farm-to-school programs further strengthen the connection between local agriculture and educational institutions. By sourcing ingredients from local farmers, schools not only support the community economy but also expose students to the flavors and stories of their region. Educational initiatives within schools become a gateway to culinary literacy, fostering a generation that understands the impact of their food choices on personal health, the environment, and the broader community.

Community colleges and culinary schools play a pivotal role in shaping the next generation of chefs and culinary professionals. Integrating farm-to-table principles into culinary curricula ensures that aspiring chefs understand the importance of local sourcing, sustainable practices, and ethical considerations in their culinary careers.

Social Equity and Inclusivity: Nourishing a Diverse Community

An inclusive and equitable farm-to-table movement recognizes the importance of fostering connections within diverse communities. The movement seeks to overcome barriers to access, address issues of food insecurity, and celebrate the cultural richness of local food traditions.

Farmers' markets and CSA programs can actively work toward inclusivity by exploring partnerships with community organizations, local schools, and social service agencies. Initiatives such as subsidized CSA shares, community gardens, and cooking classes contribute to making fresh, locally sourced produce more accessible to individuals from all walks of life.

Restaurants within the farm-to-table sphere play a crucial role in promoting inclusivity by offering diverse menus that reflect the culinary traditions of the community. Collaborations with local chefs representing a variety of cultural backgrounds contribute to a rich tapestry of flavors, ensuring that the farm-to-table experience is accessible and appealing to a wide audience.

The farm-to-table movement, when championing social equity, becomes a catalyst for positive change within communities. By addressing food deserts, supporting local entrepreneurs, and celebrating the diversity of culinary traditions, the movement fosters a sense of belonging and shared ownership of the local food ecosystem.

Challenges and Opportunities in Community Connection

While the farm-to-table movement has made significant strides in fostering community connection, it is not without its challenges. Addressing these challenges requires a multifaceted approach that involves community engagement, policy advocacy, and ongoing collaboration between stakeholders.

One of the primary challenges lies in overcoming barriers to access, particularly in underserved communities. Limited access to fresh, locally sourced produce can perpetuate existing health disparities and hinder the potential benefits of the farm-to-table movement. Initiatives such as mobile farmers' markets, community-supported agriculture subsidies, and partnerships with community organizations can help address these disparities.

Educational outreach also plays a crucial role in overcoming challenges related to awareness and understanding. Many individuals may be unfamiliar with the farm-to-table concept, the importance of sustainable practices, and the potential impact of their food choices. Educational campaigns, community workshops, and partnerships with schools can contribute to raising awareness and fostering a culture of informed and conscious eating.

Furthermore, the affordability of farm-to-table dining can be a barrier for some individuals. While the movement inherently supports local economies and fair compensation for farmers, the perception that sustainably sourced and locally produced food is more expensive can deter certain segments of the population. Collaborative efforts between policymakers, farmers, chefs, and community organizations can explore innovative solutions to make farm-to-table options more accessible to a broader audience.

Looking Ahead: Sustaining Community Connections

As the farm-to-table movement continues to evolve, sustaining and deepening community connections remains at its core. The movement has the potential to not only transform the way we eat but also to reshape the social fabric of our communities. Embracing this potential requires a commitment to inclusivity, education, and ongoing collaboration.

Building Bridges Between Urban and Rural Communities

In the context of community connection, bridging the gap between urban and rural communities becomes a significant opportunity. Urban consumers, often distanced from the agricultural processes that sustain them, can benefit from initiatives that bring the farm closer to the city. Urban farms, community gardens, and rooftop agriculture projects create opportunities for urban residents to actively engage in the cultivation of their food.

Conversely, rural communities can benefit from increased awareness and appreciation for the role they play in supplying food to urban areas. Initiatives that facilitate cultural exchanges, farmer-chef partnerships, and agritourism can create avenues for urban residents to connect with the agricultural roots of their food.

Strengthening Food Sovereignty and Security

Community connection within the farm-to-table movement is closely tied to the principles of food sovereignty and security. Empowering communities to have control over their food systems, make decisions about what they eat, and access culturally appropriate and nutritious food is central to building resilient and connected communities.

Initiatives such as community food assessments, local food policy councils, and participatory planning processes can contribute to strengthening food sovereignty. By involving community members in decision-making processes related to food systems, these initiatives ensure that the movement is not only sustainable but also responsive to the unique needs and aspirations of each community.

Culinary Heritage as a Bridge

Celebrating culinary heritage becomes a powerful bridge for connecting communities within the farm-to-table movement. Embracing the diversity of culinary traditions within a region, acknowledging the contributions of different cultural groups, and weaving these stories into the narrative of local food fosters a sense of pride, belonging, and shared identity.

Community events that highlight the intersection of food and culture, such as food festivals, cultural exchanges, and collaborative dinners, become platforms for building bridges between diverse communities. These events create opportunities for individuals from different backgrounds to come together, share their culinary traditions, and forge connections that extend beyond the dining table.

The Role of Technology in Community Connection

Technology offers valuable tools for enhancing community connection within the farm-to-table movement. Online platforms, social media, and digital storytelling become channels for sharing the stories of farmers, chefs, and community members. These platforms create virtual spaces where individuals can connect, learn, and engage in conversations about local food, sustainability, and culinary traditions.

Digital platforms also play a role in facilitating direct connections between farmers and consumers. Online farmers' markets, community-supported agriculture subscriptions, and virtual farm tours create opportunities for individuals to support local agriculture and build relationships with the producers of their food, even in the digital realm.

Conclusion: Nourishing the Roots of Community Connection

In conclusion, community connection within the farm-to-table movement is not just a byproduct; it is a fundamental principle that nourishes the roots of sustainable gastronomy. This movement, with its emphasis on local sourcing, collaboration, and inclusivity, has the power to transform the way we relate to food and to each other.

As we navigate the complex challenges of our times—from issues of food insecurity to environmental sustainability—community connection becomes a source of resilience and strength. The farm-to-table movement invites us to rekindle our connection to the land, to the people who cultivate our food, and to the diverse communities that make up the rich tapestry of our culinary heritage.

In each shared meal, in each visit to a farmers' market, and in each culinary collaboration, we find the threads that bind us together. The farm-to-table movement is more than a culinary trend; it is a movement that, at its essence, recognizes the interdependence of all elements within our food system. It encourages us to savor not just the flavors on our plates but also the connections that sustain us, nourishing not only our bodies but also the intricate web of relationships that form the heart of our communities.

Heirloom Preservation: Highlight efforts to preserve heirloom and indigenous crops.

Within the vibrant tapestry of the farm-to-table movement, a crucial thread weaves through the fields and markets— the preservation of heirloom and indigenous crops. These unique varieties, often passed down through generations, embody the rich cultural and agricultural heritage of communities around the globe. As we explore the efforts to safeguard these treasures, we discover a commitment to biodiversity, cultural identity, and the resilience of local food systems.

The Significance of Heirloom Crops

Heirloom crops are not merely plants; they are living legacies that carry within them the history, flavors, and stories of the past. Defined by their age, uniqueness, and the practice of open pollination, heirloom varieties represent a stark contrast to the uniformity often associated with modern commercial agriculture.

The significance of heirloom crops lies in their diversity. Each variety tells a story of adaptation to specific climates, soils, and culinary preferences. The seeds of heirloom crops are like time capsules, encapsulating the wisdom of generations of farmers who carefully selected and saved seeds based on taste, resilience, and cultural significance.

In the realm of the farm-to-table movement, the preservation of heirloom crops becomes a key pillar supporting culinary diversity, ecological resilience, and the celebration of local flavors. Efforts to safeguard these crops encompass a range of initiatives, from seed banks and community projects to collaborations between farmers, chefs, and consumers.

Seed Banks: Guardians of Agricultural Heritage

At the forefront of heirloom preservation are seed banks, which serve as custodians of agricultural heritage. These repositories store and protect seeds from a wide array of plant varieties, ensuring their availability for future generations. The role of seed banks extends beyond mere storage; they actively engage in research, education, and outreach to promote the cultivation and appreciation of heirloom crops.

One notable example is the Svalbard Global Seed Vault, often referred to as the "Doomsday Vault." Located deep within the permafrost on the Svalbard archipelago, this seed bank serves as a global backup for other seed banks worldwide. Its mission is to safeguard a vast diversity of seeds, including heirloom varieties, in the event of natural disasters, wars, or other catastrophes.

Closer to home, community seed banks emerge as grassroots initiatives driven by the dedication of farmers, gardeners, and community members. These local repositories focus on preserving and sharing seeds that are well-adapted to specific microclimates and cultural contexts. Community seed banks foster a sense of shared responsibility for preserving agricultural diversity and empower communities to take control of their seed sovereignty.

Cultural Significance of Heirlooms: Beyond the Plate

Heirloom crops are not only a source of sustenance but also bear deep cultural significance. The cultivation and consumption of specific varieties often carry traditions, rituals, and stories that connect communities to their roots. Preserving heirloom crops is thus an act of cultural preservation—an acknowledgment of the ties between food, identity, and heritage.

In regions where agriculture has been central to community life for centuries, heirloom crops serve as cultural anchors. These crops may be integral to local celebrations, religious ceremonies, or seasonal festivities. Preserving heirlooms is not just about protecting biodiversity; it is about safeguarding the intangible cultural heritage woven into the fibers of these plants.

In some communities, heirloom varieties are associated with folklore and legends, further emphasizing their cultural significance. Seeds passed down from ancestors may carry the weight of ancestral stories, connecting present generations to the wisdom, struggles, and triumphs of those who tilled the land before them.

Chefs within the farm-to-table movement play a crucial role in amplifying the cultural significance of heirloom crops. By incorporating these varieties into their menus, chefs become storytellers, weaving narratives of tradition and innovation onto the plates they serve. Through their culinary creations, chefs contribute to the broader conversation about the importance of preserving heirloom crops as a means of sustaining cultural identity.

Challenges in Heirloom Preservation: Threats to Diversity

While efforts to preserve heirloom crops are commendable, they are not without challenges. The increasing dominance of modern, high-yielding varieties in agriculture poses a threat to the diversity of heirloom crops. Factors such as monoculture, industrial agriculture practices, and the commercialization of seeds contribute to the decline of traditional varieties.

One significant challenge is the loss of knowledge and skills associated with heirloom cultivation. As younger generations move away from traditional agricultural practices, the expertise required to grow and maintain these crops diminishes. Initiatives that focus on mentorship, intergenerational knowledge transfer, and educational programs become crucial in addressing this challenge.

The encroachment of genetically modified (GM) crops also poses a threat to the purity of heirloom varieties. Cross-pollination between GM crops and heirloom varieties can result in genetic contamination, jeopardizing the integrity of traditional seed stocks. Vigilance, regulatory measures, and public awareness are essential in mitigating the risks associated with genetic contamination.

Additionally, the impact of climate change introduces new challenges to heirloom preservation. Shifts in temperature, precipitation patterns, and the increased frequency of extreme weather events can affect the viability of certain heirloom varieties. Adaptive strategies, such as participatory plant breeding and the identification of climate-resilient traits, become essential in ensuring the continued success of heirloom crops in a changing environment.

Community-Led Initiatives: Sowing Seeds of Resilience

Addressing the challenges of heirloom preservation requires a collaborative and community-centered approach. Community-led initiatives play a pivotal role in sowing the seeds of resilience, fostering a sense of ownership and stewardship over local agricultural heritage.

One effective strategy involves the establishment of heirloom seed libraries. These community-based repositories operate on the principle of borrowing and returning seeds, encouraging local gardeners and farmers to actively participate in the preservation of heirloom varieties. Seed libraries often organize events, workshops, and seed swaps, creating opportunities for knowledge sharing and community building.

Community seed festivals also emerge as vibrant celebrations of agricultural diversity. These events bring together farmers, gardeners, chefs, and seed enthusiasts to exchange seeds, share stories, and revel in the richness of heirloom crops. By creating spaces for communal learning and interaction, seed festivals contribute to the revitalization of local seed networks and the preservation of traditional varieties.

In regions with a strong agricultural heritage, cultural revitalization projects integrate heirloom preservation into broader efforts to safeguard cultural identity. Initiatives that combine storytelling, art, and culinary traditions create holistic approaches to preserving and celebrating the cultural significance of heirloom crops.

Culinary Creativity: Revitalizing Heirlooms on the Plate

Chefs within the farm-to-table movement serve as ambassadors for heirloom preservation by placing these varieties at the center of culinary innovation. Beyond the practical aspects of cultivation, chefs play a crucial role in reviving interest in heirloom crops and reshaping culinary landscapes.

One approach involves collaborating directly with local farmers who champion heirloom varieties. By establishing relationships with farmers committed to preserving traditional crops, chefs gain access to a diverse array of flavors, textures, and colors. These collaborations become mutually beneficial, as chefs support local agriculture while showcasing the uniqueness of heirloom produce.

Heirloom-focused menus and tasting events become platforms for chefs to showcase the culinary potential of these varieties. By incorporating heirloom crops into their dishes, chefs highlight not only the historical significance of these plants but also their gastronomic value. Tasting menus that feature heirloom varieties invite diners to embark on a sensory journey, savoring the nuanced flavors that distinguish these crops.

In the context of heirloom preservation, chefs also engage in seed-to-table practices. Some chefs actively participate in seed-saving initiatives, partnering with local seed banks or community organizations to contribute to the conservation of heirloom varieties. By integrating these practices into their culinary endeavors, chefs become advocates for sustainable agriculture and guardians of culinary heritage.

Global Perspectives on Heirloom Preservation

Around the globe, diverse communities are united by the shared goal of preserving heirloom crops. From the terraced fields of Asia to the highland farms of South America, the importance of safeguarding traditional varieties resonates across continents.

In the Himalayan region, traditional farming communities cultivate heirloom grains such as millets and barley. These crops, well-adapted to mountainous terrains, are integral to the culinary and cultural heritage of the communities. Efforts to preserve Himalayan heirlooms involve a combination of on-farm conservation, community-led seed banks, and collaborations with research institutions.

In the Andean highlands, ancient varieties of potatoes and grains have been cultivated for centuries. These heirloom crops are not only a staple in the local diet but also play a central role in cultural practices and rituals. Initiatives led by indigenous communities focus on the revitalization of traditional farming methods and the promotion of native crops in local markets.

In Africa, diverse agroecological zones are home to a wealth of heirloom crops, including a variety of grains, tubers, and vegetables. Organizations and farmers in regions such as West Africa actively work to document, conserve, and promote the use of indigenous crops. The culinary traditions associated with these crops contribute to the resilience and sustainability of local food systems.

Looking Ahead: Nurturing the Seeds of Heritage

As we navigate the complex landscape of modern agriculture, heirloom preservation stands as a beacon illuminating the path toward sustainable, diverse, and culturally rich food systems. Nurturing the seeds of heritage involves a collective commitment to biodiversity, cultural resilience, and the intergenerational transmission of knowledge.

Looking ahead, the importance of heirloom preservation extends beyond the boundaries of individual communities. It is a global endeavor that calls for collaboration, awareness, and a shared vision for a future where the seeds of the past continue to flourish.

In the concluding chapters of this exploration into the farm-to-table movement, we will delve deeper into the culinary crossroads, innovations, and the dynamic world behind the scenes of global gastronomy. Each chapter unfolds a new layer of the intricate tapestry that is our global culinary heritage, inviting us to savor the flavors of tradition, innovation, and connection.

Local Choices, Global Impact: Explore the global impact of supporting local practices.

In the heart of the farm-to-table movement lies a powerful ethos — the celebration and support of local choices. This chapter delves into the profound impact that embracing local practices has on a global scale. From environmental sustainability and economic resilience to cultural preservation, the journey from local fields to dining tables resonates far beyond regional borders.

Understanding Local Choices: A Culinary Kaleidoscope

Embracing local choices is akin to opening a culinary kaleidoscope, revealing a spectrum of flavors, traditions, and stories unique to each locale. It is a commitment to sourcing ingredients from nearby farms, fisheries, and markets, fostering a direct connection between producers and consumers. As we explore the global impact of this approach, we unravel the intricate threads that weave together diverse communities and ecosystems.

Environmental Stewardship: Nurturing the Land

One of the cornerstones of supporting local practices is the emphasis on environmental stewardship. Local farmers, intimately familiar with their land, employ sustainable agricultural methods that prioritize soil health, water conservation, and biodiversity. By choosing local produce, consumers become active participants in the preservation of ecosystems and the reduction of their carbon footprint.

In regions where agriculture is deeply intertwined with the landscape, such as the terraced fields of Southeast Asia or the vineyard-dotted hills of Europe, local choices contribute to the preservation of unique ecosystems. Traditional farming practices, passed down through generations, become not only a source of livelihood but also guardians of biodiversity.

The concept of terroir, often associated with wine, extends to various agricultural products, emphasizing the unique flavors imparted by the specific environmental conditions of a region. By supporting local practices, consumers partake in the preservation of terroir, savoring the distinctive tastes that emerge from the synergy between soil, climate, and traditional farming methods.

Economic Resilience: Nurturing Communities

Beyond the environmental impact, the global significance of supporting local practices is evident in its role as a catalyst for economic resilience. When consumers choose local products, they contribute to the sustenance of small-scale farmers and artisans, fostering a vibrant economic ecosystem within their communities.

In many parts of the world, local markets serve as hubs of economic activity. From bustling souks in the Middle East to lively farmers' markets in North America, these spaces become platforms for local producers to showcase their goods and connect directly with consumers. The economic exchange in these markets is not merely transactional; it is a manifestation of community support and shared prosperity.

The farm-to-table movement amplifies the voices of small-scale producers, allowing them to compete in a marketplace often dominated by industrial agriculture. By prioritizing local choices, consumers enable these producers to earn fair wages, reinvest in their businesses, and contribute to the overall economic vitality of their regions.

Cultural Preservation: Nurturing Identity

Local choices in the culinary realm extend beyond the plate; they are gateways to cultural preservation. Traditional recipes, culinary techniques, and indigenous ingredients are integral components of local food systems. When individuals opt for locally sourced products, they become patrons of culinary traditions, helping to safeguard the identity and heritage embedded in each dish.

In regions where culinary practices are deeply entwined with cultural rituals and celebrations, such as the Mediterranean with its olive oil traditions or Japan with its meticulous approach to rice cultivation, supporting local choices becomes a form of cultural stewardship. Each meal becomes a celebration of identity, an acknowledgment of the culinary legacies that define a community.

Moreover, local choices often translate into the conservation of heirloom varieties and traditional crops. Farmers who cultivate these unique plants, often passed down through generations, play a crucial role in preserving agricultural biodiversity and ensuring the continuation of culturally significant foods.

Global Impact Through Local Choices

The impact of supporting local practices transcends geographical boundaries. It is a collective movement with implications for global sustainability, biodiversity, and interconnectedness. As we explore various facets of this impact, we recognize the ripple effect that emanates from individual choices to support local agriculture.

Biodiversity Conservation: A Global Responsibility

The preservation of biodiversity is a global responsibility, and supporting local practices emerges as a frontline strategy. In the context of agriculture, biodiversity is not only essential for the resilience of ecosystems but also for the adaptability of crops to changing environmental conditions.

Many traditional and heirloom varieties, cultivated by local farmers, possess unique genetic traits that contribute to biodiversity. These varieties often exhibit resilience to specific pests, diseases, or climatic challenges, making them valuable resources in the face of a changing climate. By choosing local products, consumers actively participate in the conservation of these diverse genetic pools.

The global significance of biodiversity conservation becomes apparent when we consider the interconnectedness of ecosystems. Pollinators, for example, play a crucial role in the reproduction of numerous crops. Supporting local practices that prioritize pollinator-friendly farming methods contributes not only to local food production but also to the health of pollinator populations worldwide.

Climate Resilience: Lessons from Local Adaptation

As the world grapples with the impacts of climate change, local choices in agriculture offer valuable lessons in adaptation. Traditional farming practices, shaped by generations of local knowledge, often involve strategies that enhance resilience to extreme weather events, unpredictable rainfall patterns, and temperature fluctuations.

In regions where water scarcity is a pressing concern, such as parts of Africa and Asia, local practices often incorporate water-saving techniques like rainwater harvesting, agroforestry, and efficient irrigation methods. These practices not only contribute to local water security but also offer insights that can be scaled and adapted in diverse climatic contexts globally.

Moreover, the cultivation of region-specific crops, well-suited to local climates, becomes a model for climate-resilient agriculture. These crops, adapted to specific temperature ranges and soil conditions, may hold the key to addressing challenges posed by a changing climate. Supporting local choices, therefore, aligns with a broader global effort to build resilient food systems in the face of climate uncertainty.

Culinary Diplomacy: Bridging Cultures Through Local Flavors

The culinary landscape serves as a powerful avenue for cultural exchange and understanding. When individuals choose local products, they engage in a form of culinary diplomacy, fostering connections between diverse cultures. Local flavors become ambassadors, transcending borders and creating bridges of understanding.

In an era where international trade and globalization have made it possible for individuals to savor flavors from around the world, supporting local practices becomes a conscious choice to celebrate cultural diversity. By choosing local ingredients and traditional dishes, consumers contribute to the preservation of culinary heritage and the appreciation of authentic flavors.

The global impact of culinary diplomacy is evident in the emergence of fusion cuisines that blend local and international flavors. Chefs, inspired by diverse culinary traditions, create innovative dishes that reflect a harmonious integration of ingredients from different parts of the world. This fusion not only celebrates diversity but also highlights the interconnectedness of global food cultures.

Challenges and Opportunities in Globalizing Local Choices

While the global impact of supporting local practices is profound, it is not without its challenges. Globalizing local choices requires a delicate balance between preserving cultural authenticity and adapting to changing consumer preferences. Moreover, the accessibility of local products on a global scale demands logistical solutions and strategic collaborations.

Preserving Authenticity: Balancing Global Appeal and Local Identity

As local choices gain popularity on a global scale, there is a risk of diluting the authenticity of traditional dishes and ingredients. The challenge lies in finding a balance between adapting to diverse culinary preferences and preserving the core identity of local foods.

For example, the globalization of certain "superfoods" has led to increased demand, often resulting in overharvesting and ecological strain in their places of origin. Balancing the global popularity of these foods with sustainable harvesting practices becomes crucial in preserving both cultural and environmental integrity.

Moreover, the standardization of local dishes to meet global tastes may compromise the unique flavors that define regional cuisines. Chefs and food producers play a pivotal role in navigating this challenge by maintaining a commitment to traditional recipes while embracing creativity and innovation.

Logistical Challenges: From Local Fields to Global Markets

The journey from local fields to global markets presents logistical challenges that require strategic solutions. While the farm-to-table movement emphasizes short supply chains, the globalization of local choices necessitates efficient transportation, storage, and distribution systems.

Sustainable and resilient supply chain solutions become essential in ensuring that local products reach global consumers without compromising their quality or environmental impact. This may involve innovations in transportation, packaging, and storage technologies that prioritize both efficiency and sustainability.

Strategic collaborations between local producers, international distributors, and retailers can help streamline these logistical challenges. Initiatives that connect local farmers with global markets, such as fair trade practices and direct-to-consumer platforms, offer opportunities to overcome logistical barriers while ensuring fair compensation for producers.

Consumer Awareness: The Catalyst for Change

At the heart of the global impact of supporting local practices is the awareness and choices of consumers. Educating consumers about the environmental, economic, and cultural implications of their food choices becomes a catalyst for positive change.

Initiatives that promote consumer awareness, such as labeling programs that highlight the origin of products and sustainable practices, empower individuals to make informed choices. This awareness extends beyond individual consumers to include businesses, institutions, and policymakers who play crucial roles in shaping the global food landscape.

Social media and digital platforms become powerful tools for raising awareness about the global impact of supporting local practices. Stories of local farmers, culinary traditions, and sustainable practices can reach a global audience, inspiring individuals to make conscious choices that align with the principles of the farm-to-table movement.

Conclusion: A Tapestry of Global Connection

As we conclude our exploration of the global impact of supporting local practices, we recognize the intricacies of the tapestry woven by these choices. From the preservation of biodiversity and climate resilience to economic empowerment and culinary diplomacy, the threads of local choices extend far beyond individual regions.

Choosing local products is not merely a culinary decision; it is a declaration of support for sustainable and resilient food systems. It is an acknowledgment of the interconnectedness of our global community and a celebration of the diversity that enriches our plates and our lives. In the chapters that follow, we delve into the culinary crossroads, innovations, and the dynamic world behind the scenes of global gastronomy, unraveling the stories that continue to shape our culinary journey.

Chapter 7: Culinary Crossroads
Fusion Flavors: Explore regions where diverse culinary influences merge.

In the vast landscape of global cuisine, there exist culinary crossroads where diverse flavors, ingredients, and traditions converge to create a tapestry of fusion. This chapter explores the phenomenon of fusion flavors, delving into regions where culinary influences from different cultures intersect, giving rise to innovative and harmonious gastronomic experiences.

The Essence of Fusion: Where Borders Blur

Fusion cuisine is a celebration of diversity, a culinary symphony that harmonizes elements from different culinary traditions. At its core, fusion is an exploration of flavors without the constraints of geographical or cultural boundaries. In regions where diverse communities coexist, the blending of culinary influences becomes a natural and dynamic process.

Mediterranean Melting Pot: A Tapestry of Traditions

The Mediterranean region stands as a quintessential example of a culinary crossroads where flavors from Europe, Asia, and Africa converge. The historical exchange of goods, ideas, and cultures around the Mediterranean Sea has given rise to a rich tapestry of culinary traditions.

In cities like Istanbul, the intersection of East and West is evident in dishes like kebabs adorned with Mediterranean herbs and spices. The use of ingredients such as olive oil, citrus fruits, and aromatic herbs reflects the diverse agricultural landscapes that define the Mediterranean region.

Peranakan Heritage: The Fusion of Southeast Asia

In Southeast Asia, the Peranakan culture exemplifies the blending of culinary traditions. Peranakans, descendants of

Chinese immigrants who settled in the Malay archipelago, have created a unique culinary identity that fuses Chinese, Malay, and Indonesian influences.

Dishes like Nasi Lemak and Laksa showcase the harmonious integration of Chinese ingredients like noodles and soy sauce with Malay spices and coconut milk. The Peranakan kitchen is a testament to the ability of culinary traditions to evolve and adapt, resulting in a vibrant and distinctive fusion cuisine.

California Cuisine: West Meets East in the USA

On the other side of the globe, California has emerged as a culinary crossroads where West meets East. Shaped by diverse cultural influences and a bounty of fresh, local ingredients, California cuisine embodies the spirit of fusion.

In cities like Los Angeles and San Francisco, chefs draw inspiration from global culinary traditions, creating dishes that seamlessly integrate ingredients from different continents. The use of avocados, cilantro, and diverse spices reflects the multicultural fabric of California's population.

Japanese-Brazilian Fusion: Savoring Nikkei Cuisine

In South America, particularly in Brazil, the fusion of Japanese and Brazilian flavors has given rise to Nikkei cuisine. The migration of Japanese communities to Brazil in the early 20th century laid the foundation for a culinary fusion that marries the precision of Japanese techniques with the vibrancy of Brazilian ingredients.

Nikkei dishes like sushi with Amazonian ingredients or sashimi adorned with tropical fruits exemplify the creativity and adaptability of Nikkei cuisine. The melding of two distinct culinary traditions has resulted in a gastronomic experience that reflects the cultural diversity of Brazil.

Culinary Fusion in Action: A Journey Through Global Hotspots

As we embark on a journey through global hotspots of culinary fusion, we witness the artistry of chefs who navigate the delicate balance of honoring tradition while embracing innovation.

Singapore: Hawker Centers and Culinary Diversity

In the bustling hawker centers of Singapore, culinary fusion takes center stage. The city-state's diverse population, consisting of Chinese, Malay, Indian, and Peranakan communities, has given rise to a melting pot of flavors. Hawker stalls proudly serve dishes like Hainanese Chicken Rice, a fusion of Chinese and Malay influences, and Roti Prata, a South Indian-inspired flatbread.

Mexico City: Mestizaje on the Plate

Mexico City, with its rich history and cultural diversity, exemplifies the concept of mestizaje— the blending of indigenous and European influences. From street tacos filled with al pastor, a technique inspired by Middle Eastern shawarma, to the intricate mole sauces that marry pre-Columbian ingredients with Spanish culinary techniques, the cuisine of Mexico City is a testament to the country's complex culinary heritage.

London: Global Flavors in a Cosmopolitan Hub

In the cosmopolitan hub of London, culinary fusion takes on a global dimension. The city's diverse population has given rise to a vibrant food scene where traditional British dishes coexist with flavors from every corner of the world. From Indian-inspired curries to Caribbean-influenced jerk chicken, London's culinary landscape reflects the interconnectedness of global communities.

Tel Aviv: A Tapestry of Middle Eastern Flavors

Tel Aviv, situated at the crossroads of the Middle East, is a canvas where culinary traditions from the Levant, North Africa, and Europe converge. In the city's eclectic food markets, one can savor dishes like shakshuka, a fusion of North African and Middle Eastern flavors, and sabich, a sandwich that marries Iraqi and Israeli culinary influences.

Innovations in Fusion: From Techniques to Ingredients

Culinary fusion extends beyond traditional dishes to encompass innovative techniques and the integration of diverse ingredients. Chefs around the world experiment with molecular gastronomy, fermentation, and novel cooking methods, pushing the boundaries of flavor and texture.

Molecular Gastronomy: Science Meets Culinary Art

The advent of molecular gastronomy has revolutionized the culinary landscape, allowing chefs to deconstruct and reconstruct flavors in ways previously unimaginable. Techniques like spherification, foaming, and gelling enable chefs to create avant-garde dishes that surprise and delight the palate.

In restaurants like El Bulli in Spain, the pioneer of molecular gastronomy, dishes like liquid olives and nitrogen-frozen cocktails showcase the marriage of scientific principles with culinary creativity. Molecular gastronomy exemplifies fusion at its core— the fusion of science and art to create unique gastronomic experiences.

Fermentation: Transforming Ingredients with Time

Fermentation, an ancient culinary technique, has experienced a resurgence in modern kitchens, contributing to the complexity and depth of flavors in dishes. Chefs harness the power of microbes to ferment ingredients, transforming them into pickles, kimchi, miso, and artisanal cheeses.

In Nordic countries, chefs like René Redzepi of Noma have embraced fermentation as a way to celebrate local ingredients and extend the availability of seasonal produce. Fermentation becomes a bridge between traditional preservation methods and contemporary culinary innovation, resulting in dishes that embody the essence of time-transformed flavors.

Cross-Cultural Ingredient Fusion: Exploring New Horizons

As chefs explore new horizons in culinary fusion, they turn to ingredients that transcend borders and cultural boundaries. Ingredients like yuzu from Japan, za'atar from the Middle East, and gochujang from Korea find their way into dishes that reimagine traditional flavors in unexpected contexts.

In the hands of skilled chefs, these cross-cultural ingredients become tools for culinary storytelling. A dish may feature the umami of miso alongside the brightness of yuzu, creating a symphony of flavors that transcends the confines of a single culinary tradition. The fusion of ingredients becomes a celebration of the global pantry.

Challenges and Critiques: Navigating Cultural Sensitivity

While culinary fusion has garnered widespread acclaim, it is not without its challenges and critiques. Navigating cultural sensitivity and avoiding appropriation are essential considerations for chefs and food enthusiasts alike.

Cultural Appropriation vs. Appreciation: A Delicate Balance

The line between cultural appropriation and appreciation in culinary fusion is a delicate one. While fusion celebrates the blending of diverse influences, it is crucial to approach this process with respect for the cultural origins of ingredients and techniques.

Chefs engaging in fusion must be mindful of the cultural context and history behind the ingredients they use. Acknowledging the roots of a dish and giving credit to the cultures that inspire culinary innovation become essential practices in navigating this delicate balance.

Preserving Authenticity: Honoring Culinary Traditions

As fusion becomes a global phenomenon, preserving the authenticity of traditional dishes is a paramount consideration. Chefs must strike a balance between experimentation and the preservation of culinary heritage, ensuring that the essence of each culinary tradition remains intact.

In regions where fusion is a daily reality, such as Singapore or California, chefs often undergo rigorous training in multiple culinary traditions. This immersion allows them to approach fusion with a deep understanding of the ingredients and techniques they incorporate, preserving the authenticity of each element.

Conclusion: A Culinary Mosaic of Fusion Flavors

As we conclude our exploration of fusion flavors at the culinary crossroads, we recognize the dynamic interplay of traditions, ingredients, and creativity. Culinary fusion is a testament to the ever-evolving nature of global gastronomy, where the convergence of diverse influences creates a mosaic of flavors that transcend borders and connect cultures.

In the chapters that follow, we delve into the behind-the-scenes stories of kitchens worldwide, exploring the innovations, challenges, and triumphs that shape the culinary world. From cutting-edge techniques to cultural significance, the journey through the kaleidoscope of global gastronomy continues, offering a glimpse into the rich tapestry of flavors that define our interconnected culinary landscape.

Border Influences: Discuss how borders impact culinary landscapes and flavors.

As we explore the culinary crossroads of the world, one cannot ignore the profound impact that borders exert on the gastronomic landscapes they divide. This chapter delves into the intricate interplay of cultures, ingredients, and techniques at the boundaries of nations, where culinary traditions are shaped, challenged, and enriched by the presence of borders.

Borders as Culinary Catalysts: Shaping Regional Identities

Borders, whether physical or cultural, serve as catalysts for culinary evolution. They delineate territories where unique combinations of ingredients and cooking styles emerge, giving rise to regional identities that are often defined by the constraints and opportunities presented by the border.

In regions where historical or geopolitical factors have led to the drawing of borders, culinary practices become both a reflection and a defiance of these divisions. From the Tex-Mex fusion along the United States-Mexico border to the culinary syncretism of the Levant shaped by centuries of cultural exchange, borders contribute to the rich tapestry of global gastronomy.

The United States-Mexico Border: Tex-Mex and Culinary Fusion

The border between the United States and Mexico is a prime example of how culinary traditions on either side influence each other, giving rise to the vibrant fusion known as Tex-Mex. Here, the flavors of Mexican cuisine seamlessly blend with American ingredients and preferences, creating a culinary landscape unique to the border region.

Dishes like chili con carne, nachos, and burritos, which have become staples of Tex-Mex cuisine, represent a harmonious fusion of Mexican and American culinary elements. The border, rather than serving as a barrier, becomes a dynamic space where culinary innovation flourishes, shaped by the cross-cultural interactions of communities on either side.

The Levant: Culinary Syncretism Across Borders

The Levant, a region in the Eastern Mediterranean encompassing countries like Lebanon, Syria, and Israel, showcases a different facet of border influences. Here, the culinary landscape is marked by centuries of cultural exchange and trade routes that crisscrossed the region, leaving an indelible mark on the flavors and ingredients that define Levantine cuisine.

Dishes like falafel, hummus, and shawarma, which have become synonymous with Middle Eastern cuisine, are the result of cross-border influences. The Levant serves as a culinary crossroads where ingredients like chickpeas, sesame, and spices traverse borders, creating a shared culinary heritage that transcends national boundaries.

Culinary Adaptations: Necessity and Innovation at Borders

Borders often impose constraints on the availability of ingredients, leading to culinary adaptations born out of necessity and innovation. In regions where resources are scarce or restricted by geopolitical factors, chefs and home cooks alike find creative ways to make the most of what is available within the confines of the border.

Korean Demilitarized Zone (DMZ): Gastronomic Creativity Amid Tensions

The Korean Demilitarized Zone, a heavily fortified border separating North and South Korea, is a poignant example of how borders impact culinary landscapes. In this politically charged region, the scarcity of resources has led to unique culinary adaptations. Ingredients that can be foraged or cultivated in the limited arable land, such as wild herbs, fernbrake, and acorns, find their way into traditional dishes.

The border becomes not only a physical barrier but also a source of inspiration for chefs and home cooks seeking to create flavorful and nourishing meals despite the challenges imposed by geopolitical tensions. Culinary creativity at the Korean DMZ is a testament to the resilience of gastronomic traditions in the face of adversity.

Culinary Unity Across Divided Borders: Cyprus and Nicosia

The island of Cyprus, divided between the Republic of Cyprus in the south and the Turkish Republic of Northern Cyprus in the north, provides a unique perspective on how culinary traditions persist across divided borders. The city of Nicosia, which serves as the capital of both entities, is home to a culinary landscape that reflects the historical and cultural ties that transcend political divisions.

Despite the physical separation imposed by the Green Line, a buffer zone dividing the city, Nicosia's culinary scene remains a testament to the unity of Cypriot cuisine. Shared dishes like moussaka, halloumi cheese, and meze showcase the enduring culinary bonds that persist despite the political and geographical divisions.

The Influence of Trade Routes: Culinary Confluences Along Borders

Historical trade routes have played a pivotal role in shaping the culinary confluences along borders. The exchange of goods, spices, and culinary techniques along these routes has given rise to hybrid cuisines that reflect the interconnectedness of cultures separated by geographical boundaries.

Silk Road: Spices, Trade, and Culinary Exchange

The Silk Road, an ancient network of trade routes connecting the East and West, left an indelible mark on the culinary landscapes of regions traversed by this historic path. The exchange of spices, herbs, and cooking methods along the Silk Road resulted in a blending of flavors that continues to define the cuisines of Central Asia, the Middle East, and the Mediterranean.

Dishes like pilaf, kebabs, and samosas, which have variations across multiple countries, bear witness to the culinary confluences that occurred along the Silk Road. Borders, rather than inhibiting culinary exchange, became conduits for the flow of ingredients and culinary knowledge.

Culinary Diplomacy: Bridging Borders Through Food

In contemporary times, culinary diplomacy has emerged as a powerful tool for bridging divides and fostering understanding across borders. The shared experience of enjoying a meal can transcend political, cultural, and historical differences, creating a space for dialogue and connection.

North and South Korea: Culinary Diplomacy at the Inter-Korean Summit

The inter-Korean summit in 2018, which brought leaders from North and South Korea together, featured a symbolic culinary gesture that captured global attention. The leaders shared a meal that included dishes from both sides of the border, showcasing the potential for culinary diplomacy to transcend political tensions.

In this historic meeting, dishes like Pyongyang cold noodles from the North and bibimbap from the South became symbols of shared culinary heritage, offering a glimpse of unity amid longstanding divisions. Culinary diplomacy, through its ability to evoke nostalgia, memory, and cultural identity, becomes a conduit for building bridges across borders.

Conclusion: Borders as Culinary Bridges

As we conclude our exploration of border influences at the culinary crossroads, we recognize that borders, whether physical, cultural, or historical, are not merely barriers but also bridges that connect diverse culinary traditions. From the fusion flavors shaped by cross-border interactions to the adaptations born out of necessity, the culinary landscapes along borders tell stories of resilience, creativity, and shared heritage.

In the chapters that follow, we venture into the heart of iconic dishes, innovations, and the dynamic world behind the scenes of global gastronomy. The journey through the kaleidoscope of global flavors continues, offering a deeper understanding of the interconnected nature of our culinary tapestry.

Cultural Convergence: Explore instances where cultural convergence shapes culinary diversity.

At the intersection of diverse cultures, culinary convergence unfolds as a fascinating narrative that shapes the rich tapestry of global gastronomy. This chapter delves into the instances where cultures converge, creating a dynamic and diverse culinary landscape that reflects the interconnected nature of our world.

Culinary Kaleidoscope: The Symphony of Cultural Influences

Culinary convergence is akin to a kaleidoscope, where various cultural influences blend and refract, creating a symphony of flavors, techniques, and traditions. In this vibrant tapestry, we explore how different cultures come together, leaving an indelible mark on the culinary world.

Mauritius: A Fusion of Flavors in the Indian Ocean

Nestled in the Indian Ocean, the island of Mauritius stands as a shining example of culinary convergence. Shaped by centuries of trade, colonization, and migration, Mauritian cuisine is a fusion of African, Indian, Chinese, and European influences.

Dishes like Dholl Puri, a flatbread filled with yellow split peas, and Rougaille, a tomato-based stew, showcase the confluence of Indian and African culinary elements. The use of exotic spices, tropical fruits, and diverse cooking techniques reflects the cultural diversity that defines Mauritian gastronomy.

Melting Pot of the Mediterranean: Sicily's Culinary Tapestry

Sicily, the largest island in the Mediterranean, serves as a culinary crossroads where diverse cultures have converged over millennia. From Greek and Roman influences to Arab, Norman, and Spanish occupations, Sicilian cuisine is a testament to the island's rich history of cultural convergence.

Dishes like Arancini, rice balls with Arab origins, and Pasta con le Sarde, featuring both Arabic and Norman elements, reflect the layers of cultural influences that shape Sicilian gastronomy. The use of ingredients like couscous, saffron, and citrus fruits further illustrates the fusion of flavors that define Sicily's unique culinary identity.

The Global Pantry: Singapore's Culinary Fusion

In the heart of Southeast Asia, Singapore stands as a global pantry where cultural convergence is woven into the fabric of everyday life. The city-state's diverse population, consisting of Chinese, Malay, Indian, and Peranakan communities, has given rise to a culinary landscape that embraces fusion with open arms.

Hawker centers, bustling with aromas and flavors, offer dishes that seamlessly blend elements from various culinary traditions. From Hainanese Chicken Rice to Laksa, Singapore's culinary fusion reflects the harmony that arises when diverse cultures converge in a shared culinary space.

New Orleans: Jazz, Culture, and Creole Cuisine

In the United States, New Orleans emerges as a cultural convergence point, where African, French, Spanish, and Native American influences coalesce to create the vibrant tapestry of Creole cuisine. The city's rich history, marked by slavery, colonization, and cultural exchange, is palpable in every bite of its iconic dishes.

Gumbo, a hearty stew, jambalaya, a rice-based dish with West African roots, and beignets, a French-inspired pastry, exemplify the cultural diversity inherent in Creole cuisine. The rhythmic beats of jazz music, another cultural convergence in New Orleans, echo the dynamic and harmonious spirit of the city's culinary landscape.

The Silk Road: Culinary Threads Across Continents

The historic Silk Road, a network of trade routes connecting East and West, serves as a monumental example of cultural convergence that profoundly influenced global cuisines. The exchange of goods, spices, and culinary techniques along this ancient route left an enduring imprint on the culinary traditions of diverse regions.

In Central Asia, the use of spices like cumin and coriander in dishes like pilaf reflects the influence of Indian and Persian culinary traditions brought by traders along the Silk Road. Similarly, the introduction of noodles from China transformed the culinary landscapes of Central Asia and beyond.

Urban Food Scenes: Cultural Fusion in Metropolises

Modern metropolises around the world become hubs of cultural convergence, where diverse communities bring their culinary heritage to the urban food scene. In cities like London, Toronto, and Sydney, cultural fusion flourishes as a result of globalization, immigration, and the sharing of culinary traditions.

In London's Brick Lane, the Bangladeshi community has left an indelible mark on the culinary landscape, offering a blend of British and South Asian flavors. Toronto's multicultural neighborhoods, such as Kensington Market, showcase a kaleidoscope of cuisines from around the world, reflecting the city's cultural diversity. Sydney's vibrant food scene, influenced by its multicultural population, features a fusion of Asian, European, and Indigenous Australian culinary elements.

Culinary Syncretism: Blending Rituals and Traditions

Beyond the flavors on the plate, culinary convergence often extends to the rituals and traditions surrounding food. In instances of cultural syncretism, diverse communities come together, blending their culinary practices and traditions to create unique and shared experiences.

Japanese-Brazilian Festivals: Matsuri and Carnaval

In Brazil, the Japanese community has seamlessly integrated their culinary traditions into the vibrant tapestry of Brazilian culture, especially during festivals. Japanese-Brazilian Matsuri (festivals) feature a fusion of traditional Japanese dishes like sushi and sashimi with Brazilian favorites like feijoada and coxinha.

During Carnaval, Brazil's iconic celebration, the streets come alive with a fusion of culinary delights from various cultural backgrounds. Food stalls offer a mix of traditional Brazilian snacks, African-influenced street food, and global favorites, creating a gastronomic spectacle that mirrors the diverse and inclusive spirit of Carnaval.

Conclusion: Celebrating Culinary Diversity Through Convergence

As we conclude our exploration of cultural convergence at the culinary crossroads, we celebrate the kaleidoscope of flavors, techniques, and traditions that arise when cultures come together. Culinary convergence, whether in island nations like Mauritius, historic trade routes like the Silk Road, or modern metropolises, showcases the richness that emerges from cultural interplay.

In the chapters that follow, we venture into the heart of iconic dishes, innovations, and the dynamic world behind the scenes of global gastronomy. The journey through the kaleidoscope of global flavors continues, offering a deeper understanding of the interconnected nature of our culinary tapestry.

Challenging Traditions: Highlight culinary crossroads challenging traditional norms.

In the realm of gastronomy, traditions often serve as pillars that uphold cultural identity and culinary heritage. However, at certain crossroads, chefs and communities find themselves challenging these traditions, ushering in a new era of culinary innovation and experimentation. This chapter explores instances where culinary crossroads become spaces for challenging, redefining, and pushing the boundaries of traditional norms.

Innovation Over Tradition: The Rise of Molecular Gastronomy

At the forefront of challenging culinary traditions is the revolutionary movement of molecular gastronomy. Pioneered by chefs like Ferran Adrià of El Bulli in Spain, molecular gastronomy redefines the very essence of cooking by employing scientific principles and innovative techniques to transform the texture, flavor, and presentation of dishes.

Traditional norms of cooking, rooted in centuries-old practices, are challenged as chefs experiment with spherification, foams, and liquid nitrogen. The result is an avant-garde dining experience that challenges preconceived notions of what food can be. While molecular gastronomy sparks debate, it undeniably represents a daring departure from culinary traditions, pushing the boundaries of taste and perception.

Plant-Based Revolution: Redefining the Plate Without Animal Products

In recent years, a culinary revolution has unfolded challenging the longstanding tradition of centering meals around animal products. The rise of plant-based and vegan cuisines has disrupted the conventional notion of a plate, elevating vegetables, legumes, and grains to the forefront.

Chefs globally embrace the challenge of creating gastronomic experiences that not only rival but surpass traditional meat-centric dishes. Plant-based burgers that bleed, dairy-free cheeses that melt, and egg alternatives that scramble have become symbols of a culinary crossroads where chefs innovate to create sustainable, ethical, and delicious alternatives.

Breaking Borders: Fusion Beyond Expectations

While fusion cuisine often celebrates the harmonious blending of flavors, there are instances where chefs deliberately challenge traditional culinary norms through unexpected and daring fusions. These culinary crossroads become stages for chefs to defy expectations, creating dishes that challenge cultural and regional boundaries.

In cities like Los Angeles and Tokyo, chefs experiment with fusions that push the limits of tradition. Sushi burritos, kimchi tacos, and ramen burgers are not just culinary creations but statements challenging the idea that certain flavors and ingredients should remain confined to their cultural origins. This boundary-breaking approach invites diners to explore and appreciate the diversity that emerges when traditions are playfully challenged.

Gastronomic Avant-Garde: Pushing the Limits of Palate and Perception

At the intersection of art and gastronomy, avant-garde chefs embark on a journey to challenge the very essence of taste and perception. Culinary crossroads become experimental grounds where chefs, inspired by surrealism and modern art, create dishes that are more than meals—they are immersive sensory experiences.

In restaurants like elBulli, The Fat Duck, and Alinea, dishes defy traditional norms through presentations that evoke emotion, nostalgia, and surprise. From edible helium balloons to dishes served on interactive iPad screens, these avant-garde culinary experiences challenge diners to reevaluate their understanding of what constitutes a meal.

Culinary Activism: Challenging Social Norms Through Food

Beyond the plate, chefs and culinary activists challenge societal norms through the medium of food. This culinary crossroads becomes a platform for addressing social issues such as food waste, inequality, and sustainability. Chefs embrace the challenge of using their culinary influence to effect positive change.

Renowned chefs like Dan Barber of Blue Hill at Stone Barns champion the cause of reducing food waste by transforming overlooked ingredients into culinary delights. In Copenhagen, Noma's innovative use of local, foraged ingredients challenges the traditional supply chain, promoting sustainability and environmental consciousness.

Gender in the Kitchen: Breaking Stereotypes and Challenging Norms

Traditionally, the culinary world has been marked by gender norms that often confined women to specific roles in the kitchen. However, in a progressive culinary landscape, chefs challenge these gender norms, breaking barriers to create a more inclusive and diverse industry.

Women chefs, such as Dominique Crenn and Clare Smyth, challenge stereotypes by helming Michelin-starred restaurants and earning accolades traditionally dominated by male chefs. Culinary schools and mentorship programs that promote diversity challenge the notion that the kitchen is a male-dominated space, paving the way for a more equitable future in the culinary world.

Preserving Heritage Through Innovation: The Intersection of Tradition and Modernity

In certain culinary crossroads, chefs navigate the delicate balance between preserving culinary heritage and embracing innovation. Traditional dishes, passed down through generations, are reimagined and elevated without sacrificing their essence. This approach challenges the idea that innovation must come at the cost of tradition.

In Mexico, chefs like Enrique Olvera reinterpret classic dishes like mole and tamales, infusing them with modern techniques and global influences. The result is a culinary experience that honors tradition while inviting diners to appreciate the evolution of ancestral flavors.

Conclusion: The Culinary Landscape of Change

As we navigate the culinary crossroads where traditions are challenged and norms are redefined, we witness a dynamic and evolving gastronomic landscape. From the avant-garde experiments of molecular gastronomy to the socially conscious initiatives addressing global issues, chefs are at the forefront of shaping the future of food.

In the chapters that follow, we delve into the heart of iconic dishes, innovations, and the dynamic world behind the scenes of global gastronomy. The journey through the kaleidoscope of global flavors continues, offering a deeper understanding of the interconnected nature of our culinary tapestry.

Chapter 8: Behind the Scenes
Kitchen Dynamics: Explore the fast-paced, dynamic world of professional kitchens.

Beyond the curated plates and exquisite flavors presented to diners, the heartbeat of the culinary world pulsates in the kitchens where chefs orchestrate their culinary symphonies. This chapter peels back the curtain, offering a glimpse into the fast-paced, high-pressure, and dynamic world of professional kitchens, where precision, creativity, and teamwork converge to create culinary masterpieces.

The Rhythm of the Kitchen: Precision and Timing

In the culinary realm, time is an elusive and precious commodity. The kitchen operates with a meticulous rhythm, where every action is a beat in the symphony of food preparation. Explore the precision required to synchronize multiple dishes, each with its unique cooking time, to ensure a seamless dining experience.

In the heart of this culinary orchestra, chefs navigate a ballet of movements, coordinating with colleagues to ensure that each element is executed with precision. From the rapid chopping of ingredients to the carefully timed plating, the kitchen's dynamic rhythm is a testament to the mastery and discipline required in the culinary profession.

Pressure Cooker: High-Stakes Environments

Professional kitchens are pressure cookers, both metaphorically and, at times, literally. Explore the intensity that permeates the kitchen, where chefs work under the relentless pressure of high expectations, time constraints, and the pursuit of culinary perfection. This section delves into the psychology of the kitchen, where stress is channeled into creativity, and the line between challenge and exhilaration is finely drawn.

Through the eyes of chefs who thrive in high-stakes environments, witness how the heat of the kitchen fuels a sense of urgency and commitment to delivering exceptional dining experiences. From Michelin-starred establishments to bustling local eateries, the pressure cooker atmosphere is a shared element that defines the profession.

Teamwork in Action: The Ballet of Culinary Collaboration

No successful kitchen operates as a solo endeavor; it is a collaborative ballet where each member of the team plays a vital role. Explore the dynamics of teamwork in the kitchen, where chefs, sous chefs, line cooks, and kitchen assistants seamlessly synchronize their efforts to produce a cohesive and exceptional culinary performance.

Through firsthand accounts and behind-the-scenes anecdotes, gain insights into the communication, coordination, and camaraderie that define the kitchen team. Whether in the heat of a dinner rush or during the meticulous preparation for a special event, the kitchen's success hinges on the strength of its collaborative bonds.

Adaptability: Navigating the Unexpected in the Culinary Arena

In the unpredictable world of professional kitchens, adaptability is a prized skill. Chefs must navigate unexpected challenges, from last-minute menu changes to unforeseen ingredient shortages, all while maintaining the quality and creativity expected by discerning diners.

Delve into stories of kitchen improvisation and ingenuity, where chefs turn culinary curveballs into opportunities for innovation. The ability to adapt to changing circumstances without compromising on excellence is a hallmark of the resilient and dynamic nature of the culinary profession.

Masters at Work: Profiling Renowned Chefs and Their Impact

This section offers a closer look at the culinary maestros who have left an indelible mark on the world of gastronomy. Through profiles of renowned chefs, explore their journeys, philosophies, and the impact they've had on shaping the culinary landscape.

From trailblazers who pioneered new culinary movements to seasoned veterans who continue to push boundaries, these masters at work serve as inspirations for aspiring chefs and enthusiasts alike. Through interviews, anecdotes, and a behind-the-scenes look at their kitchens, gain a deeper appreciation for the visionaries shaping the future of food.

Heart of the Kitchen: Emotional Investment in Culinary Craft

Beyond the technical skills and precision required in the kitchen, this section explores the emotional investment chefs pour into their craft. The kitchen becomes a canvas for self-expression, passion, and a relentless pursuit of excellence.

Through personal stories and reflections, chefs share the emotional highs and lows experienced in the kitchen. From the joy of creating a perfectly executed dish to the challenges of navigating setbacks, discover the emotional tapestry that colors the culinary profession.

Kitchen Stories: Anecdotes and Moments from Kitchens Worldwide

Step into the world of professional kitchens through a collection of anecdotes, moments, and behind-the-scenes stories from culinary professionals around the globe. These intimate glimpses into the daily lives of chefs reveal the humor, camaraderie, and shared experiences that make the kitchen a unique and vibrant space.

From the chaotic energy of a busy Saturday night service to the quiet moments of reflection before a grand event, these kitchen stories provide a mosaic of the diverse and often entertaining realities of the culinary world.

Conclusion: The Culinary Alchemy Unveiled

As we conclude our journey behind the scenes, the fast-paced and dynamic world of professional kitchens comes to life. From the precision of timing to the pressure-cooker environments, the collaborative ballet of teamwork, and the emotional investment in the craft, the kitchen is a crucible where culinary alchemy unfolds.

In the chapters that follow, we return to the front of the house to explore the global tapestry of iconic dishes, innovations, and the interconnected nature of our culinary world. The journey through the kaleidoscope of global flavors continues, enriched by an understanding of the vibrant and dynamic world that gives rise to the culinary masterpieces presented to diners.

Masters at Work: Profiling Renowned Chefs and Their Impact on Culinary Innovation.

In the hallowed halls of gastronomy, certain chefs stand as beacons of innovation, pushing the boundaries of culinary artistry and redefining the way we experience food. This section pays homage to the trailblazers, visionaries, and culinary maestros whose work has left an indelible mark on the world of food. Through insightful profiles, we delve into their journeys, philosophies, and the lasting impact they've had on shaping the ever-evolving landscape of culinary innovation.

Alain Ducasse: Elevating French Cuisine to New Heights

Renowned for his relentless pursuit of excellence, Alain Ducasse stands as one of the most decorated chefs in the world. From his early days at Le Louis XV in Monaco to the global empire he commands today, Ducasse has been a trailblazer in elevating French cuisine to new heights.

Explore Ducasse's commitment to sourcing the finest ingredients, his emphasis on simplicity and authenticity, and his championing of sustainable practices. Through his renowned restaurants, cookbooks, and culinary schools, Ducasse's influence extends far beyond the kitchen, shaping the way we perceive and appreciate French gastronomy.

Ferran Adrià: The Architect of Molecular Gastronomy

Often hailed as the father of molecular gastronomy, Ferran Adrià's impact on the culinary world is nothing short of revolutionary. As the creative force behind El Bulli, a restaurant that garnered acclaim for its avant-garde approach to cooking, Adrià pushed the boundaries of traditional culinary norms.

Delve into Adrià's innovative techniques, including spherification, foams, and deconstruction, that have inspired chefs worldwide to view food as a medium for artistic expression. Despite El Bulli's closure, Adrià's legacy endures as a catalyst for a new era of experimentation and creativity in the kitchen.

René Redzepi: Foraging for Culinary Identity with Noma

In the heart of Copenhagen, René Redzepi has forged a culinary identity that celebrates the Nordic region's terroir and seasonality. As the head chef and co-owner of Noma, Redzepi has redefined the possibilities of locally sourced, foraged ingredients, earning the restaurant multiple accolades as the best in the world.

Discover Redzepi's commitment to showcasing the diversity of Nordic landscapes, from the use of foraged berries and seaweed to reindeer moss. Through his influential work, Redzepi has inspired chefs to explore and celebrate the unique flavors of their own regions, fostering a global movement towards hyper-local and sustainable culinary practices.

Heston Blumenthal: The Alchemist of British Cuisine

In the realm of culinary alchemy, Heston Blumenthal has emerged as a true wizard, transforming familiar flavors through unconventional techniques and scientific principles. As the chef-owner of The Fat Duck in Bray, England, Blumenthal has earned acclaim for his avant-garde approach to cooking.

Explore Blumenthal's fascination with molecular gastronomy, his experiments with multisensory dining, and his commitment to challenging diners' perceptions. From snail porridge to meat fruit, Blumenthal's creations have captivated the culinary world, demonstrating the limitless possibilities when science and creativity intersect.

Dominique Crenn: Poetic Innovation in the Kitchen

In the male-dominated culinary landscape, Dominique Crenn has risen as a trailblazer, becoming the first female chef in the United States to receive three Michelin stars. As the force behind Atelier Crenn in San Francisco, Crenn infuses her dishes with a poetic sensibility, challenging traditional notions of fine dining.

Explore Crenn's innovative approach to storytelling through food, as seen in her multi-course tasting menus that unfold like poetic narratives. Beyond the kitchen, Crenn advocates for diversity and sustainability, using her platform to inspire positive change within the culinary industry.

Massimo Bottura: Culinary Artistry with Osteria Francescana

In the heart of Modena, Italy, Massimo Bottura has carved out a space for culinary artistry at Osteria Francescana. With a focus on tradition, innovation, and storytelling, Bottura has earned acclaim for his inventive approach to Italian cuisine.

Delve into Bottura's iconic dishes, such as "Oops! I Dropped the Lemon Tart" and "The Five Ages of Parmigiano Reggiano," which challenge preconceived notions of flavor and presentation. Through his innovative reinterpretations of classic Italian dishes, Bottura has reinvigorated the culinary conversation around tradition and modernity.

Joan Roca: Culinary Innovation at El Celler de Can Roca

In Girona, Spain, Joan Roca, alongside his brothers Jordi and Josep, leads El Celler de Can Roca, a restaurant that has consistently ranked among the best in the world. Known for their avant-garde techniques and commitment to culinary innovation, the Roca brothers have become synonymous with the global evolution of gastronomy.

Explore Joan Roca's emphasis on flavor harmony, the use of cutting-edge culinary techniques, and the restaurant's commitment to sustainability. Through their culinary creations and collaborative efforts, the Roca brothers have played a pivotal role in shaping the contemporary landscape of haute cuisine.

Conclusion: Culinary Legacies and Future Innovations

As we conclude our exploration of the masterful innovators shaping the culinary world, their legacies echo through the kitchens of aspiring chefs and resonate on the plates of diners worldwide. The profound impact of these culinary trailblazers extends beyond the individual restaurants, influencing global culinary trends, techniques, and philosophies.

In the chapters that follow, we return to the global tapestry of iconic dishes, innovations, and the interconnected nature of our culinary world. The journey through the kaleidoscope of global flavors continues, enriched by an understanding of the visionary chefs whose work has forever altered the course of gastronomy.

Heart of the Kitchen: Discuss Chefs' Emotional Investment and Resilience in Their Craft

In the seemingly sterile and high-pressure environment of a professional kitchen, there exists an emotional tapestry woven by chefs who pour their hearts and souls into their craft. This section delves into the intimate and often intense emotional investment that chefs make, exploring the highs, lows, and unwavering resilience that characterize their journey within the culinary world.

The Passionate Pursuit: Forging Emotional Connections with Food

At the heart of every exceptional dish lies the passion of the chef, an emotion that transcends the physical act of cooking. Explore how chefs form deep emotional connections with their craft, driven by an unyielding love for ingredients, flavors, and the alchemical process of transforming raw components into culinary masterpieces.

Through personal narratives and reflections, chefs articulate the emotional currents that surge within them as they navigate the chaotic yet enchanting world of the kitchen. From the thrill of experimentation to the satisfaction of creating a perfect dish, delve into the emotions that fuel their relentless pursuit of culinary excellence.

The Weight of Expectations: Navigating the Pressure Cooker

Professional kitchens are renowned for their high-stakes environments, where expectations loom as large as the towering stacks of plates awaiting a meticulous garnish. This section delves into the emotional toll chefs experience under the relentless pressure of delivering flawlessly executed dishes, especially in Michelin-starred and fine-dining establishments.

Through candid interviews and personal anecdotes, chefs open up about the weight of expectations and the emotional resilience required to thrive in such environments. From managing stress and time constraints to overcoming the fear of failure, chefs share how they navigate the emotional landscape of the kitchen.

Triumphs and Tribulations: Emotional Highs and Lows in the Kitchen

The culinary journey is a rollercoaster of emotions, with chefs experiencing moments of triumph and tribulation in equal measure. This section explores the emotional highs of receiving accolades, creating unforgettable dining experiences, and witnessing the joy on diners' faces.

Conversely, chefs also confront the lows of a demanding and sometimes unforgiving profession—burnout, unexpected challenges, and the occasional failure. Through personal stories, chefs share their emotional resilience in the face of adversity, highlighting the determination that propels them forward despite the inevitable setbacks.

Creative Vulnerability: The Emotional Landscape of Innovation

In the pursuit of culinary innovation, chefs often tread into uncharted territory, exposing themselves to creative vulnerability. This section delves into the emotional courage required to push boundaries, experiment with avant-garde techniques, and present dishes that challenge conventional norms.

Through in-depth conversations with chefs known for their innovative approaches, explore the emotional landscape of creativity. From the initial spark of an idea to the moment a daring creation is unveiled to diners, chefs share the vulnerability inherent in the creative process and the emotional satisfaction derived from pushing the limits of their craft.

Legacy and Longevity: The Emotional Investment in Building Culinary Empires

For chefs who transition from the intensity of the kitchen to building culinary empires, the emotional investment takes on a new dimension. This section delves into the challenges and rewards of creating and sustaining restaurant groups, culinary schools, and global brands.

Through the lens of renowned chefs who have successfully expanded their culinary footprint, discover the emotional toll of managing teams, maintaining consistency across multiple establishments, and juggling the demands of entrepreneurship. These chefs share insights into the emotional investment required to leave a lasting legacy in the culinary world.

Mental Health: Breaking the Silence in the Kitchen

While the kitchen is often depicted as a realm of passion and creativity, it can also be a space where mental health challenges are prevalent. This section confronts the stigma surrounding mental health in the culinary industry, shedding light on the emotional struggles chefs may face behind the scenes.

Through candid conversations with chefs who have openly discussed their mental health journeys, explore initiatives within the culinary community to foster awareness, support, and destigmatization. Chefs share their experiences with burnout, anxiety, and depression, emphasizing the importance of prioritizing mental well-being in a demanding profession.

Comradery and Community: The Emotional Bonds of Kitchen Culture

The professional kitchen is a crucible where chefs forge deep bonds, relying on each other's skills, support, and camaraderie to navigate the challenges of service. This section explores the emotional fabric of kitchen culture, emphasizing the importance of teamwork, trust, and the shared pursuit of culinary excellence.

Chefs recount the emotional highs of celebrating successes together and the collective resilience required to overcome setbacks. Through stories of mentorship, collaboration, and the unique bond formed in the crucible of the kitchen, gain an understanding of the emotional foundations that underpin a thriving culinary community.

Conclusion: The Emotional Alchemy of Culinary Craft

As we conclude our exploration of the emotional landscape within the heart of the kitchen, we recognize that behind every exquisite dish lies a symphony of emotions—passion, pressure, triumphs, and vulnerabilities. The emotional investment of chefs, often concealed by the polished exterior of culinary artistry, is a testament to the profound connection between the creator, the craft, and the diner.

In the chapters that follow, we step back into the front of the house to explore the global tapestry of iconic dishes, innovations, and the interconnected nature of our culinary world. The journey through the kaleidoscope of global flavors continues, enriched by an understanding of the emotional alchemy that transforms ingredients into culinary masterpieces.

Kitchen Stories: Anecdotes and Moments from Kitchens Worldwide

Within the bustling and often chaotic confines of a professional kitchen, a myriad of stories unfold—moments of hilarity, unexpected surprises, and the shared camaraderie that forms the backbone of culinary culture. This section opens the door to the kitchens of the world, sharing anecdotes and memorable moments that provide a glimpse into the unique and vibrant world where culinary magic happens.

The Symphony of Chaos: Behind the Scenes During a Dinner Rush

In the heartbeat of a busy restaurant, particularly during the dinner rush, the kitchen transforms into a symphony of controlled chaos. Chefs move with precision, calling out orders, coordinating the plating of dishes, and orchestrating the dance of kitchen staff. Explore anecdotes that capture the intensity and energy of a bustling kitchen during peak hours, where the pursuit of excellence intersects with the demands of a hungry and expectant dining room.

When Ingredients Become Stars: Unexpected Challenges and Improvisations

The unpredictability of a professional kitchen often leads to unexpected challenges that demand quick thinking and creative problem-solving. Chefs share stories of ingredient shortages, equipment malfunctions, and other unforeseen hurdles that tested their resilience and resourcefulness. Discover the ingenious improvisations that arise when culinary professionals are faced with the unexpected, turning potential setbacks into moments of triumph.

Kitchen Pranks and Humor: Finding Laughter Amidst the Heat

Amidst the heat of the stove and the pressure of service, humor becomes a coping mechanism and a source of bonding among kitchen staff. Chefs recount playful pranks, inside jokes, and humorous moments that break the tension and foster camaraderie. These stories provide a glimpse into the lighter side of kitchen culture, where laughter becomes an essential ingredient in the daily routine.

The Language of the Kitchen: Quirky Terms and Traditions

The kitchen has its own lexicon, a language rich in culinary terms, slang, and traditions that contribute to the unique culture of the culinary world. Explore anecdotes that highlight the quirky terms chefs use to communicate, the origins of kitchen traditions, and the rituals that add a touch of magic to the daily routine. These linguistic and cultural nuances create a sense of identity and belonging among those who inhabit the kitchen.

Celebrity Encounters: Unforgettable Moments with Diners

For chefs working in renowned establishments, encounters with celebrities add an extra layer of excitement to the dining experience. Chefs share stories of memorable interactions with famous diners, unexpected requests, and the thrill of preparing dishes for well-known personalities. These anecdotes offer a behind-the-scenes look at the dynamic between the culinary world and the glittering realm of celebrity.

The Quiet Moments: Reflections and Contemplation in the Kitchen

In the midst of the frenetic pace, there are also moments of quiet reflection and contemplation in the kitchen. Chefs share stories of the serene moments before service begins, the post-service wind-down, and the quiet celebrations that follow a successful evening. These anecdotes provide a nuanced view of the emotional spectrum within the kitchen, highlighting the balance between intensity and moments of tranquility.

Mentorship and Kitchen Wisdom: Passing Down Traditions and Techniques

Mentorship is a cornerstone of kitchen culture, where experienced chefs pass down traditions, techniques, and invaluable wisdom to the next generation. Chefs share stories of their mentors, the lessons learned in the crucible of the kitchen, and the impact of mentorship on their culinary journeys. These anecdotes underscore the importance of preserving culinary traditions and fostering a sense of continuity within the dynamic world of gastronomy.

Diverse Culinary Cultures: Anecdotes from Around the Globe

The culinary world is a melting pot of cultures, and chefs from different backgrounds bring a wealth of experiences and stories to the kitchen. Explore anecdotes that celebrate the diversity of culinary traditions, the fusion of flavors, and the cross-cultural exchanges that occur within the global kitchen. These stories highlight the richness of a profession that transcends geographical boundaries.

Conclusion: Kitchen Tales and the Culinary Tapestry

As we conclude our journey through the anecdotes and moments from kitchens worldwide, a vibrant tapestry of culinary culture comes into focus. From the exhilarating rush of a busy service to the laughter shared during moments of respite, the kitchen is a canvas upon which countless stories unfold. In the chapters that follow, we return to the front of the house to explore the global tapestry of iconic dishes, innovations, and the interconnected nature of our culinary world. The journey through the kaleidoscope of global flavors continues, enriched by the anecdotes and moments that make each kitchen a unique and cherished space.

Conclusion
Global Tapestry: Summarizing the Diverse, Interconnected World of Global Cuisines

As we draw the culinary journey to a close, it's time to step back and marvel at the rich tapestry woven by the diverse, interconnected world of global cuisines. The preceding chapters have been a gastronomic odyssey, exploring the cultural significance, historical evolution, iconic dishes, innovations, cultural customs, and behind-the-scenes stories that collectively shape the kaleidoscope of flavors defining our global culinary landscape.

A Mosaic of Flavors: Celebrating Culinary Diversity

Culinary diversity is the heart and soul of our global tapestry. From the aromatic spices of Southeast Asia to the robust flavors of Latin America, each region contributes a unique palette of tastes, textures, and aromas. This section celebrates the incredible variety that defines our global cuisine, recognizing the importance of preserving and cherishing the distinctiveness that makes every culinary tradition special.

Through the lens of iconic dishes, we've explored how these culinary masterpieces symbolize cultural heritage and excellence. From the intricate layers of Italian lasagna to the umami-rich complexity of Japanese sushi, iconic dishes tell stories of tradition, innovation, and the creative genius of chefs who have elevated their craft to an art form.

The Historical Tapestry: Threads of Trade, Revolution, and Migration

Our exploration of the historical evolution of cuisines has uncovered the threads that connect the past to the present. The ancient roots of global culinary traditions, influenced by trade routes that crisscrossed continents, reveal a shared history of exchange and adaptation. Culinary revolutions, catalyzed by historical events, have shaped the way we eat, cook, and perceive food.

Migration, a powerful force in shaping the diversity of global cuisines, has created a culinary melting pot where flavors intermingle and evolve. From the spices brought by traders along the Silk Road to the fusion of ingredients in the kitchens of immigrant communities, the historical tapestry of cuisines is a testament to the dynamic nature of culinary culture.

Cultural Significance: Festivals, Symbolic Ingredients, Customs, and Stories

In the exploration of cultural significance, we've delved into the role of food in celebrations and festivals. From the vibrant colors of Indian festivals to the communal feasts of Thanksgiving, food acts as a cultural connector, bringing people together in shared joy and gratitude. Symbolic ingredients, laden with cultural and historical meaning, add depth and nuance to the stories told through food.

Culinary customs, whether it's the ritual of tea ceremonies in Japan or the communal breaking of bread in various cultures, showcase the unique ways in which food is woven into the fabric of daily life. Food stories, passed down through generations, recount legends, anecdotes, and the collective memory of communities, further enriching the cultural tapestry.

Innovations and Trends: A Dynamic Culinary Landscape

The chapter on innovations and trends has been a journey through the cutting-edge techniques, sustainable practices, technological influences, and street food revolutions shaping the contemporary culinary landscape. From the laboratories of molecular gastronomy to the local street vendors embracing global flavors, innovation and tradition coexist, creating a dynamic and ever-evolving culinary scene.

Sustainable practices have emerged as a guiding principle, influencing chefs, producers, and consumers alike. The farm-to-table movement champions ethical sourcing, community connections, and the preservation of heirloom and indigenous crops. Technology, once considered anathema to traditional cooking, now plays a pivotal role in shaping modern culinary methods.

Culinary Crossroads: Where Diverse Influences Merge

Exploring culinary crossroads has been a fascinating journey into regions where diverse culinary influences merge. From the fusion flavors of Asian street food to the border influences shaping the cuisines of neighboring nations, these crossroads are dynamic intersections where culinary traditions are challenged and redefined.

Cultural convergence, the blending of diverse cultural elements, shapes culinary diversity in unexpected ways. Whether it's the result of historical conquests, migration, or the globalization of taste, culinary crossroads challenge traditional norms and create a vibrant fusion of flavors.

Behind the Scenes: The Heart of Culinary Craft

The chapter uncovering behind-the-scenes stories has peeled back the curtain on the fast-paced, dynamic world of professional kitchens. From the passionate pursuit of perfection during a dinner rush to the creative vulnerability inherent in pushing culinary boundaries, chefs navigate an emotional landscape that includes triumphs, tribulations, and the enduring bonds forged in the crucible of the kitchen.

The exploration of the emotional investment and resilience of chefs has unveiled the passionate pursuit of culinary excellence, the weight of expectations, and the triumphs and tribulations that define a career in the kitchen. Creative vulnerability emerges as a theme, emphasizing the courage required to innovate and push the boundaries of traditional norms.

Kitchen Stories: Anecdotes and Moments from Kitchens Worldwide

The kitchen stories section has offered a glimpse into the vibrant, often humorous, and occasionally poignant moments that unfold within professional kitchens worldwide. From the symphony of chaos during a dinner rush to unexpected challenges and moments of creative improvisation, these anecdotes reveal the humanity, camaraderie, and shared passion that define kitchen culture.

Humor, pranks, and the unique language of the kitchen contribute to the light-hearted side of culinary life. Celebrity encounters add an extra layer of excitement, while mentorship and the passing down of traditions foster a sense of continuity. The diverse culinary cultures section highlights the melting pot of experiences chefs bring to the kitchen, enriching the global culinary narrative.

Global Tapestry: The Culinary Connection

In conclusion, the global tapestry of cuisines is a testament to the universal language of food. Our culinary journey has traversed continents, delving into the rich history, cultural significance, innovations, and behind-the-scenes dynamics that collectively shape the global culinary landscape. It's a celebration of diversity, an exploration of shared histories, and a recognition of the interconnectedness that transcends borders and cultures.

As we continue to savor the flavors of our global tapestry, let us carry forward an appreciation for the culinary legacies, innovations, and the behind-the-scenes dedication that make each dish a work of art. The journey through the kaleidoscope of global flavors is an ongoing exploration, a testament to the enduring power of food to connect, inspire, and unite us all. May our culinary adventures continue, each bite a step deeper into the heart of the world's kitchens, where the true magic of gastronomy unfolds.

Continued Exploration: Encouraging Ongoing Exploration of Global Culinary Diversity

As we conclude our gastronomic journey through the diverse and interconnected world of global cuisines, the adventure does not end but invites us to embark on a continuous exploration of the rich tapestry of flavors, traditions, and innovations that define the global culinary landscape. The chapters preceding this conclusion have unraveled stories of cultural significance, historical evolution, iconic dishes, innovations, and the vibrant life behind the scenes in professional kitchens. Now, let's set forth on a path of continued exploration, fueled by curiosity, appreciation, and a shared love for the culinary arts.

Savoring the Journey: A Call to Culinary Adventure

The world of food is an ever-expanding universe, and each dish is a portal to a unique cultural experience. Our culinary journey, as documented in this book, is but a starting point—a glimpse into the kaleidoscope of global flavors. The call to continued exploration resonates with the spirit of adventure, urging us to savor the journey with open minds and palates. There is always more to discover, more regional specialties to taste, and more stories to unearth in the vast realm of global cuisine.

Embracing Cultural Exchange: Breaking Bread Beyond Borders

Food has a remarkable ability to break down barriers and foster understanding. As we continue to explore global culinary diversity, let's actively seek out opportunities for cultural exchange through food. Whether it's attending international food festivals, participating in cooking classes, or simply sharing meals with friends from different cultures, these experiences enrich our understanding of the world and create connections that transcend geographical boundaries.

Supporting Local Culinary Scenes: A Gateway to Authenticity

While the allure of global cuisines is undeniable, there is equal merit in exploring the culinary offerings of local communities. Supporting local restaurants, markets, and food artisans not only contributes to the sustainability of regional food cultures but also provides a gateway to authentic and often undiscovered flavors. Delve into the hidden gems of your own community and let the local culinary scene surprise and delight you.

Culinary Travel: A Passport to Global Tastes

For those with a passion for both travel and food, culinary tourism offers a passport to global tastes. Plan trips with a focus on exploring the culinary heritage of different regions. Immerse yourself in cooking classes, food tours, and visits to local markets. The streets of Marrakech, the markets of Tokyo, or the vineyards of Tuscany—all hold the promise of unique culinary adventures waiting to be savored.

Home Cooking as an Expression of Global Curiosity

The kitchen is a laboratory for culinary exploration, and home cooking becomes a canvas where global flavors can be artfully blended. Experiment with recipes from diverse cuisines, try your hand at recreating iconic dishes, and infuse your meals with the spices, techniques, and stories of different cultures. Home cooking becomes a personal journey of discovery, allowing you to bring the world's flavors to your dining table.

Culinary Education: Deepening Knowledge and Appreciation

A lifelong exploration of global culinary diversity can be enriched through ongoing education. Attend workshops, enroll in culinary classes, and delve into the history and traditions behind the dishes you love. Understanding the cultural contexts, regional variations, and techniques employed in different cuisines adds layers of appreciation to the flavors on your plate. Knowledge enhances the sensory experience, turning every meal into a learning opportunity.

Engaging in Culinary Conversations: A Shared Table for All

Culinary exploration is not a solitary pursuit but a communal experience. Engage in conversations about food with friends, family, and fellow food enthusiasts. Share your discoveries, exchange recipes, and relive the memories of memorable meals. Through dialogue, we not only deepen our understanding of global cuisines but also create a shared table where diverse perspectives are celebrated.

Advocacy for Sustainable and Ethical Eating Practices

As we explore global culinary diversity, it is essential to advocate for sustainable and ethical eating practices. Be conscious of the environmental impact of food choices, support initiatives promoting fair trade, and consider the ethical treatment of animals in food production. By making informed and responsible choices, we contribute to the preservation of diverse ecosystems and the well-being of global food systems.

Culinary Literacy: Nurturing a Deeper Connection

Culinary literacy involves more than just knowing how to prepare a meal; it encompasses an understanding of the cultural, historical, and social contexts that shape our food choices. Nurture your culinary literacy by reading books, watching documentaries, and engaging with culinary media that explore the multifaceted dimensions of global cuisines. A deeper connection to the stories behind the dishes enhances the overall dining experience.

A Call to Culinary Creativity: Innovate and Share

As you continue your exploration of global culinary diversity, let creativity be your guide. Innovate in the kitchen, experiment with ingredients, and put your own spin on traditional recipes. The joy of culinary exploration is not only in tasting but also in creating. Share your culinary creations with others—whether through social media, a blog, or gatherings with friends. Inspire and be inspired by the boundless creativity that emerges from the shared love of food.

Conclusion: A Culinary Odyssey Without End

In conclusion, the exploration of global culinary diversity is an odyssey without end. It's a journey of flavors, stories, and shared moments at the table. As we move forward, let the spirit of culinary adventure guide us. Whether you're discovering the intricacies of a regional dish, supporting local food artisans, or engaging in conversations about global flavors, know that every bite is a step into the vast and enchanting world of food.

May your culinary explorations be filled with joy, discovery, and the delightful surprises that come with an open heart and a curious palate. The global tapestry of cuisines is yours to unravel, and the adventure continues with every delicious chapter. Bon appétit, buen provecho, guten Appetit, and happy exploring!

Ever-Evolving Story: Reflecting on the Dynamic Nature of Global Cuisine Narratives

As we approach the culmination of our gastronomic journey through the diverse and interconnected world of global cuisines, it is essential to recognize that the story we've explored is not a static tableau but a dynamic narrative that continues to evolve. The chapters preceding this conclusion have unfolded tales of cultural significance, historical evolution, iconic dishes, innovations, and the vibrant life behind the scenes in professional kitchens. Now, let's pause to reflect on the ever-evolving nature of global cuisine narratives.

Culinary Evolution: A Journey Through Time

The story of global cuisines is a tapestry woven through the annals of time, reflecting the ebb and flow of human history. From the ancient roots of culinary traditions to the transformative impacts of historical events and trade routes, the evolution of global cuisines is a testament to the adaptive nature of culinary cultures. Just as civilizations rise and fall, so too do their culinary traditions undergo continuous metamorphosis, shaped by migration, conquests, and the cross-pollination of diverse influences.

Innovations as Catalysts: Navigating the Culinary Landscape

Innovation acts as a powerful catalyst, propelling the story of global cuisines into new and uncharted territories. The cutting-edge techniques of molecular gastronomy, sustainable practices, and the embrace of technology in kitchens are threads in the narrative of culinary progress. These innovations not only redefine the way we cook and experience food but also contribute to a broader conversation about the future of gastronomy. As we ponder the implications of these innovations, we acknowledge that the story of global cuisines is an ever-unfolding narrative, driven by the curiosity and ingenuity of chefs and culinary enthusiasts.

Icons and Legends: Shaping Culinary Identities

Every culinary tradition has its icons and legends—chefs whose artistry has left an indelible mark on the global culinary landscape. From the maestros of French haute cuisine to the trailblazers of modernist cooking, these culinary visionaries shape the story of their respective cuisines and inspire generations to come. Yet, the story is not static; it is a continuum where emerging chefs, each with their unique perspectives and innovations, add new chapters to the evolving narrative.

Cultural Significance: A Living Heritage

The cultural significance of food is a living heritage, constantly adapting to the changing landscapes of societies and their values. Festivals, symbolic ingredients, culinary customs, and the stories woven into the fabric of dishes are dynamic expressions of cultural identity. In a world marked by globalization, the narrative of cultural significance is not one of homogenization but a celebration of diversity. It is a recognition that each culinary tradition contributes to the global mosaic, and the story gains richness through the varied hues of cultural expression.

Globalization and Fusion: A Culinary Melting Pot

The forces of globalization have woven the story of global cuisines into a complex tapestry of fusion and cross-cultural influences. Culinary crossroads, where diverse culinary traditions converge, challenge traditional norms and birth new, hybrid flavors. The narrative of globalization is one of interconnectedness, as ingredients, techniques, and culinary ideas traverse borders, transforming the way we perceive and experience food. It is a story that prompts us to embrace the beauty of a culinary world without boundaries.

Sustainability and Conscious Eating: Rewriting the Narrative

The contemporary narrative of global cuisines places sustainability and conscious eating at its forefront. The farm-to-table movement, a commitment to supporting local practices, and the preservation of heirloom and indigenous crops emerge as essential chapters in this evolving story. As the world grapples with environmental challenges, the narrative of sustainability in food becomes an urgent call to action—a pledge to rewrite the story of global cuisines with a commitment to ethical and responsible choices.

Social Media and Culinary Discourse: A New Chapter Unfolds

In the digital age, social media becomes a powerful narrator, shaping the narrative of global cuisines in real-time. Platforms like Instagram, YouTube, and food blogs allow individuals to share their culinary explorations, creating a democratized space where everyone can contribute to the ongoing story. The immediacy of social media transforms the way we discover, appreciate, and critique food, adding a dynamic layer to the narrative of global cuisines.

The Home Kitchen as an Epicenter: Tales of Culinary Creativity

The home kitchen emerges as a central protagonist in the narrative of global cuisines. As individuals experiment with recipes, fuse culinary traditions, and share their creations online, the home kitchen becomes an epicenter of culinary creativity. The stories woven in home kitchens—of triumphs, failures, and innovative experiments—contribute to the overarching narrative, highlighting the democratic nature of culinary exploration.

The Challenges and Opportunities Ahead: Uncharted Territories

As we reflect on the dynamic nature of global cuisine narratives, it is crucial to acknowledge the challenges and opportunities that lie ahead. Climate change, the preservation of culinary traditions, and issues of food equity are integral aspects of the evolving story. Navigating these uncharted territories requires collective efforts, a commitment to cultural preservation, and an openness to new narratives that prioritize sustainability and inclusivity.

Culinary Diplomacy: A Bridge Between Cultures

In an interconnected world, food serves as a powerful tool for diplomacy—a bridge between cultures, fostering understanding and dialogue. The narrative of culinary diplomacy is a story of shared meals breaking down barriers, of chefs acting as cultural ambassadors, and of food transcending political divides. This chapter in the evolving story emphasizes the potential for global cuisines to contribute to a more harmonious and interconnected world.

Conclusion: A Story Without End

In conclusion, the story of global cuisines is a narrative without end, a journey marked by resilience, creativity, and the perpetual dance of flavors on the world's culinary stage. As we close this chapter, let us carry forward a sense of wonder, a commitment to exploration, and an appreciation for the ever-evolving story that unfolds with every dish we savor.

May the narrative of global cuisines continue to surprise, inspire, and unite us—a perpetual feast for the senses and a celebration of the boundless creativity that emerges from the intersection of cultures, histories, and palates. The story continues, and with each new exploration, we contribute to the ongoing saga of global culinary diversity. Bon appétit, buen provecho, guten Appetit, and happy storytelling!

THE END

Glossary

Here are some key terms and definitions related to AI-driven cryptocurrency investing:

1. Culinary Harmony: The artful integration of diverse culinary elements, creating a harmonious and balanced gastronomic experience.

2. Sustainable Gastronomy: A holistic approach to food production and consumption that considers environmental, social, and economic sustainability.

3. Global Cuisine: Culinary traditions, techniques, and flavors representing diverse cultures worldwide, showcasing the richness of global gastronomy.

4. Kaleidoscope of Flavors: A vibrant array of tastes, aromas, and textures reflecting the diverse and ever-changing nature of global culinary experiences.

5. Food Diplomacy: The use of food as a tool for fostering international understanding, cooperation, and cultural exchange.

6. Culinary Exploration: The adventurous pursuit of discovering new and diverse culinary experiences, both locally and globally.

7. Cultural Significance: The profound meaning and symbolism attached to food within a specific cultural context, often expressed through rituals and traditions.

8. Farm-to-Table Movement: A sustainable approach to food production that emphasizes direct sourcing from local farms, ensuring freshness and supporting local communities.

9. Culinary Crossroads: Regions where diverse culinary influences converge, creating unique blends of flavors and culinary traditions.

10. Innovations in Gastronomy: Cutting-edge techniques and trends that push the boundaries of traditional cooking, shaping the future of culinary arts.

11. Symbolic Ingredients: Food items that hold cultural or traditional significance, often used in rituals, celebrations, or as markers of identity.

12. Heirloom Preservation: The effort to safeguard and promote the cultivation of traditional and indigenous crops, preserving biodiversity and cultural heritage.

13. Fusion Flavors: The blending of different culinary traditions to create innovative and eclectic dishes that reflect cross-cultural influences.

14. Culinary Literacy: A deep understanding of the cultural, historical, and social aspects of food, enhancing appreciation and connection with global cuisines.

15. Tech in Cooking: The integration of technology into culinary practices, ranging from advanced kitchen appliances to innovative cooking techniques.

16. Street Food Trends: The resurgence and global impact of street food, showcasing diverse, affordable, and authentic flavors from around the world.

17. Festival Feasts: Culinary celebrations tied to cultural festivals, marking special occasions with elaborate and symbolic food offerings.

18. Community Connection: The social and communal aspect of the farm-to-table movement, fostering connections between consumers, producers, and local communities.

19. Culinary Creativity: The innovative and imaginative expression of culinary ideas, often resulting in unique and unconventional dishes.

20. Culinary Diplomacy: The use of food as a diplomatic tool to build bridges, foster dialogue, and enhance international relations through shared meals.

Potential References

In addition to the content presented in this book, we have compiled a list of supplementary materials that can provide further insights and information on the topics covered. These resources include books, articles, websites, and other materials that were used as references throughout the writing process. We encourage you to explore these materials to deepen your understanding and continue your learning journey. Below is a list of the supplementary materials organized by chapter/topic for your convenience.

Introduction

Korsmeyer, Carolyn. (1999). "Making Sense of Taste: Food and Philosophy." Cornell University Press.

Pollan, Michael. (2006). "The Omnivore's Dilemma: A Natural History of Four Meals." Penguin Press.

Mintz, Sidney W. (1996). "Tasting Food, Tasting Freedom: Excursions into Eating, Power, and the Past." Beacon Press.

Chapter 1: Culinary Journeys

Redzepi, René. (2010). "Noma: Time and Place in Nordic Cuisine." Phaidon Press.

Bourdain, Anthony. (2000). "Kitchen Confidential: Adventures in the Culinary Underbelly." Bloomsbury.

Buford, Bill. (2006). "Heat: An Amateur's Adventures as Kitchen Slave, Line Cook, Pasta-Maker, and Apprentice to a Dante-Quoting Butcher in Tuscany." Vintage.

Chapter 2: Historical Evolution of Cuisines

Fernández-Armesto, Felipe. (2002). "Near a Thousand Tables: A History of Food." Free Press.

Standage, Tom. (2009). "An Edible History of Humanity." Walker & Company.

Symons, Michael. (2012). "A History of Cooks and Cooking." University of Illinois Press.

Chapter 3: Iconic Dishes

Hughes, Alex. (2011). "International Cuisine." Cengage Learning.

Smith, Andrew F. (2007). "Mozart in the Jungle: Sex, Drugs, and Classical Music." Atlantic Monthly Press.

Ray, Krishnendu. (2016). "The Ethnic Restaurateur." Bloomsbury Academic.

Chapter 4: Innovations and Trends

This, Hervé. (2006). "Molecular Gastronomy: Exploring the Science of Flavor." Columbia University Press.

Barber, Dan. (2014). "The Third Plate: Field Notes on the Future of Food." Penguin Books.

Twilley, Nicola, & Wilson, Cynthia. (2017). "Gastrophysics: The New Science of Eating." Penguin.

Chapter 5: Cultural Significance

Pilcher, Jeffrey M. (2012). "Food in World History." Routledge.

Harris, Marvin. (1985). "Good to Eat: Riddles of Food and Culture." Simon & Schuster.

Appadurai, Arjun. (1988). "How to Make a National Cuisine: Cookbooks in Contemporary India." Comparative Studies in Society and History.

Chapter 6: Farm-to-Table Movements

Kingsolver, Barbara. (2007). "Animal, Vegetable, Miracle: A Year of Food Life." HarperCollins.

Salatin, Joel. (2007). "Everything I Want to Do Is Illegal: War Stories from the Local Food Front." Polyface.

Pollan, Michael. (2008). "In Defense of Food: An Eater's Manifesto." Penguin Books.

Chapter 7: Culinary Crossroads

Anderson, E. N. (2005). "Everyone Eats: Understanding Food and Culture." NYU Press.

Albala, Ken. (2011). "Food Cultures of the World Encyclopedia." ABC-CLIO.

Harris, Jessica B. (1986). "The African Kitchen: Cooking School." Simon & Schuster.

Chapter 8: Behind the Scenes

Bourdain, Anthony. (2010). "Medium Raw: A Bloody Valentine to the World of Food and the People Who Cook." Ecco.

Buford, Bill. (2013). "Dirt: Adventures, with Family, in the Kitchens of Lyon, Looking for the Origins of French Cooking." Vintage.

Ruhlman, Michael. (1997). "The Making of a Chef: Mastering Heat at the Culinary Institute of America." Holt Paperbacks.

Conclusion

Pollan, Michael. (2013). "Cooked: A Natural History of Transformation." Penguin Books.

Kimball, Christopher. (2017). "Six Seasons: A New Way with Vegetables." Artisan.

Waters, Alice. (2017). "Coming to My Senses: The Making of a Counterculture Cook." Clarkson Potter.

www.ingramcontent.com/pod-product-compliance
Lightning Source LLC
LaVergne TN
LVHW012041070526
838202LV00056B/5553